A Guide to
Electronic
Music

A Guide to
Electronic
Music

PAUL GRIFFITHS

THAMES AND HUDSON

First published in the United States
by Thames and Hudson, Inc., 1980
500 Fifth Avenue
New York, New York 10110

Library of Congress Catalog Card Number: 79–5159

Text set in 10/12 pt VIP Sabon, printed and bound
by Haddon Craftsmen, Inc.

Printed in the U.S.A.

ISBN 0 500 01224 5 cloth
     0 500 27203 4 paper.

1 2 3 4 5 6 7 8 9 0

Contents

for Michael Gerzon

I Introductions

I.1 Orientation

The material of music is sound, as that of painting is light, and yet most of our music makes use only of very narrowly defined selections from the enormous range of sounds we can hear. The entire literature of piano music, from the sonatas of Haydn to those of Boulez, requires an instrument which can produce no more than eighty or so pitches, while the palette of instruments available to the composer, though comparatively variegated in the modern symphony orchestra, again confines his imagination in quite particular ways.

Restriction, of course, has its benefits in demanding subtlety and in encouraging a continuity of tradition: the whole development of western music might well have been impossible without the standardization imposed on permissible sounds. Yet for centuries there have been musicians and writers who dreamt of the riches that lay beyond the boundaries. Francis Bacon, writing at the time of Monteverdi, speaks in surprisingly modern terms of the music of his 'New Atlantis': 'We have sound houses where we practise and demonstrate all sounds and their generation. We have harmonies ... of quarter sounds and lesser slides of sounds.' The great liberation of the electronic medium is that it enables the composer to emulate and to excel the musicians of the New Atlantis, that it makes it possible for him to use any sound whatever. Only the physiological sensitivity of the listener's ear, and the artistic sensitivity of the composer's, prescribe limits to the possible.

Microphones and tape recorders can capture, and so make available for composition, the wealth of sounds existing in the natural world, from the rustle of leaves to human speech, from a violin note to the noise of a slamming door, including also sounds which are barely if at all audible to the unaided ear. Moreover, electronic equipment can be used to create a universe of sounds never heard, new sounds made quite artificially or else by the transformation of natural ones. And, with the aid of computer technology, these new sounds can be determined in fine detail. Alternatively, electronic devices can be used in live performance in a variety of ways, alone or in conjunction with conventional musical instruments. The possibilities are endless, and their very abundance can be an embarrassment to the composer: alongside the great works of electronic music there is much that fails for want of a competent handling of the medium, a sufficient sureness of aim and technique.

The purpose of this book is to provide a guide to important achievements and to suggest means of approach. Only music with a significant electronic component is considered here, but that category includes a major part of avant-garde music produced since the second world war, and there is every reason to believe that the contribution of electronics to contemporary music will grow. Certainly it is no longer possible to dismiss electronic music as an esoteric sideline. As the second and largest part of this guide will show, much has been done in widely different fields of interest; the third part includes a select list of recordings with brief notes on those composers who have achieved most in the medium. But first the map of a history and the compass of criteria.

I.2 Retrospect

The development of electronic music has depended from its outset on an even-handed interplay between technological and creative advances. No electronic music would have been possible without the discovery, which came with Alexander Graham Bell's telephone of 1876, that sounds can be converted into electrical signals and back again. The invention of the gramophone, which swiftly followed, established the possibility of storing and altering sounds. But in the age of Wagner, Brahms and Bruckner it was unlikely that any compositional use would be made of these new and still primitive devices. The birth of electronic music had to await not only refinements in the equipment but also the coming of a mental atmosphere is which radical musical experiment might seem feasible.

That happened during the years from 1890 to 1914 or there-abouts, at which time composers as diverse as Debussy and Mahler, Bartók and Schoenberg, Webern and Strauss were rapidly extending the range of sounds which could be admitted into music. Schoenberg's breakthrough into atonality, which came about in 1908, suggested that any combination of pitches could be used, that there need be no favouring of the tonal harmonies which had been music's foundation since the Renaissance. Debussy, in particular, brought a new approach to instrumental colour as something of integral importance, not merely a musical dressing. And the greater responsibility of the percussion section in, for example, Mahler's later symphonies was also significant, for 'noise' (i.e. unpitched) instruments now began to assume a function above that of emphasis or decoration. All these advances, notably demonstrated together in such a work as Webern's Five Orchestral Pieces (1911–13), implied a kind of adventurousness which might find the electronic medium, with its greatly enlarged variety of sounds, a fruitful field.

Beginnings: electronic instruments

During this period of musical ferment, early in 1906, Thaddeus Cahill exhibited in Holyoke, Massachusetts, his 'dynamophone' or 'telharmonium', the first instrument to make music by electrical means. It apparently weighed two hundred tons, and it generated sounds from dynamos, transmitting them over telephone wires. Nothing now remains of this dinosaur of electronic music apart from a couple of faded photographs, but the path had been opened, and the new vistas were quickly recognized by such an unlikely musical revolutionary as Ferruccio Busoni. Writing in his *Sketch for a New Aesthetic of Music* (1907), he seized on Cahill's invention as foreshadowing the way out of the impasse he had detected in western music. 'Exhaustion', he wrote, 'surely waits at the end of a course the longest lap of which has already been covered. Whither then shall we turn our eyes? In what direction does the next step lead? To abstract sound, to unhampered technique, to unlimited tonal material.'

But that still could be only a distant vision. The next step towards electronic music came with the gradual development during the years up to 1915 of the valve oscillator, eventually perfected by the prolific American inventor Lee De Forest. The oscillator, which remains a basic device in electronic sound-generating equipment, made it possible to produce pitched tones from electrical signals and so to construct more manageable electronic instruments. Leon Termen, a Russian scientist better known under the gallicized name of 'Thérémin', developed the first of these in 1919–20. Further refined during the twenties, his instrument, the theremin, used an oscillator which was remotely controlled by the motions of the performer's hands around a vertical aerial.

Other electronic instruments swiftly followed. The German inventor Jörg Mager introduced several during the twenties, and in 1931 was commissioned to create electronic bell sounds for the Bayreuth production of *Parsifal*. The ondes martenot of the Frenchman Maurice Martenot and the trautonium of the German Friedrich Trautwein both appeared in 1928, and in 1929 the American Lorens Hammond produced the first electric organ. All these instruments, more sophisticated than the original theremin, enabled the performer to control timbre as well as pitch and volume. Electric organs tended to be regarded as substitutes for pipe instruments, at least until Stockhausen and other young composers began to write for them in the sixties, but the novel qualities of the ondes martenot and the trautonium held an immediate appeal for some composers. Messiaen wrote for an ensemble of six ondes martenot in his *Fête des belles eaux* (1937) and used the instrument as a soloist in his *Trois petites liturgies de la Présence Divine* (1944) and *Turangalîla-symphonie* (1946–8); it was also used by Honegger, Jolivet, Boulez and others, gaining a repertory large enough to ensure its survival. Hindemith and Strauss both composed for the trautonium, and Varèse had two instruments specially built by Termen for his *Ecuatorial* (1934), later replacing these with ondes martenot.

Further steps: records, radio, film

The electronic instruments of the twenties and thirties, though they enjoyed something of a vogue, did not come anywhere near providing all the benefits which composers expected from the new technology. They might allow music to push further towards the extremes of audible pitch; they might introduce new colours to the orchestra; but they were hardly the means for a musical revolution.

Varèse, who had known Busoni at the time when the latter was writing his *Sketch for a New Aesthetic of Music*, was the most vocal and the most far-sighted in calling for radically new tools. 'I refuse', he said in a newspaper interview as early as 1916, 'to submit myself to sounds that have already been heard. What I am looking for are new technical mediums which can lend themselves to every expression of thought and can keep up with that thought.'

It seemed likely that the promised land might be reached through the manipulation of sounds on gramophone records, and several composers, including Milhaud, Hindemith and Varèse himself, made experiments between the wars with discs on variable-speed turntables, which could bring about limited but still striking transformations. Meanwhile the Italian futurist writer Marinetti approached electronic music from a different direction in his wordless radio dramas, bringing together diverse recorded sounds in suggestive collages. John Cage, also working for the broadcast medium, used test records of pure frequency tones, which he played on variable-speed turntables, in his *Imaginary Landscape no. 1* (1939), and then, in *Imaginary Landscape no. 2* (1942), he pioneered live electronic music by using among his sound sources an amplified coil of wire.

Other composers of the time, at first in France and at the Bauhaus, investigated the potential of the film soundtrack as a creative medium, one which had the advantage over the disc that it could be handled easily, but the disadvantage that the results were difficult to control. A soundtrack records sounds in patterns of light and dark on a transparent strip beside the frames of the film, so that one can create sounds on it by, for example, drawing designs on an unused strip, though without full certainty about what will emerge. Even so, techniques of this kind were developed around 1940 by Norman McLaren, a Canadian working in New York, and by the brothers James and John Whitney in Hollywood.

Varèse at this time hoped that the film companies might take a lead in promoting electronic music. In 1940 he wrote to a Hollywood producer outlining his ideas: 'Why not startle the imagination into a realization of the reality of the unfolding drama (whether of nature or of human lives) by the use of combinations of sound possible today but which never before today could have been produced? ... It seems to me that the motion picture industry might profit (even in the dollar sense in the end) in having a laboratory or a department for the study of the problem of a more complete and understanding use of the sound apparatus'. But this was not to be; Hollywood found its profits more readily in other directions.

The dawn: 'musique concrète'

The first laboratory for electronic music was instituted not, as Varèse had hoped, at a film studio but at a radio station. Pierre Schaeffer, a sound technician working for Radio-diffusion-Télévision Française, in 1948 extended earlier work with discs to produce several short studies in what he called 'musique concrète'. Each of his pieces was based on sounds from a particular source, such as railway trains or the piano, and the recordings were transformed by his playing them at different speeds, forwards or in reverse, isolating fragments and superimposing one sound on another. It was Schaeffer's aim thus to free his material from its native associations, and he made the important discovery that this could be done very simply by removing the opening instants of a sound (the 'starting transient' as it is called). A bell stroke, for example, deprived of its beginning sounds more like an organ note.

Schaeffer's early studies were broadcast by RTF on 5 October 1948 in what was billed as a 'concert of noises'. The result was immediate interest from the public and from fellow composers: electronic music had at last arrived. Several young musicians visited Schaeffer's studio, one of them, Pierre Henry, remaining to collaborate with him on the first major work of *musique concrète*, the *Symphonie pour un homme seul*, which received its premiere during the first public concert of electronic music, given at the Ecole Normale de Musique in Paris on 18 March 1950. In 1951 the studio was formally established as the Groupe de Musique Concrète and opened to other composers. Messiaen came to create his only work in the new medium, *Timbres-durées* (1952), and his pupils Boulez, Stockhausen and Barraqué, among others, all produced studies. Their interest was, however, short-lived: they left disenchanted by Schaeffer's emphasis on using recordings rather than electronically generated sounds, and also by his lack of concern with their pursuance of serial thought and new approaches to musical form.

By now the arrival of the tape recorder, invented in 1935 but not widely available until around 1950, had transformed the practice of working with sounds in the studio. All the processes which Schaeffer had used in his early disc studies were now made much simpler, since a sound could readily be isolated on a piece of magnetic tape; there was no need for the array of discs and turntables with which the first examples of *musique concrète* had been laboriously composed.

One of the first composers to benefit from this was, appropriately enough, Varèse who in 1953 received the gift of a tape recorder after pressing for just such means for more than thirty years. He immediately began gathering sound material for an electronic piece, and in 1954 arrived at the Paris studio to complete the work which emerged as *Déserts*, alternating sections of *musique concrète* with passages for an orchestra of wind and percussion. The work was given its first performance in Paris on 2 December 1954, in a concert which was one of the earliest to be broadcast in stereo. The result was an outburst similar to that which, forty years earlier, had greeted *The Rite of Spring*, for Varèse, by placing electronic music within the context of an orchestral composition, had implied that the new medium was to be considered seriously as an extension of the old, not kept to the esoteric confines of 'concerts of noises'.

A new dawn: 'Elektronische Musik'

The second leading European studio for electronic music was founded in 1952 at the Cologne station of Nordwestdeutscher Rundfunk (later Westdeutscher Rundfunk) by Herbert Eimert, soon joined by Stockhausen. In opposition to the principles of *musique concrète*, Eimert and Stockhausen set out to create what they called '*Elektronische Musik*', music generated exclusively by electronic means, without using natural sources of sound: their work proceeded from that carried out earlier in Cologne by Werner Meyer-Eppler and Robert Beyer, who developed an instrument, the melochord, for producing sound from oscillators and other electronic devices. This emphasis on 'pure' electronic music went together with a desire to generalize the serial method introduced by Schoenberg in the early twenties. Where Schoenberg had confined the technique to the domain of pitch, basing his works on twelve-note series which were arrangements of the chromatic scale, Eimert and Stockhausen sought to extend serial organization to every aspect of sound, encompassing duration, volume and timbre. The electronic medium seemed uniquely suited to such endeavours, since it allowed the composer to gauge quantities exactly, and since there appeared to be no reason why any sound could not be constructed from the basic atoms of pure frequencies obtained from oscillators.

It is necessary at this point to refer back to the pioneering work in the physics of sound conducted by Hermann von Helmholtz, whose book *On the Sensations of Tone as a Physiological Basis for the Theory of Music* (1863) laid the foundations of modern acoustics. Helmholtz, completing earlier work by Joseph Sauveur, concluded that the timbre of a note, the quality which distinguishes a middle C played on the clarinet from the same note on the piano, depends on contributions from frequencies other than that of the basic pitch. When middle C is played on the piano, for instance, the hammered string vibrates at a rate of 256 cycles per second, corresponding to the pitch of middle C, but it also bears and gives rise to other frequencies of vibration. An oscillator, on the other hand, can be made to produce just the single pure frequency, often referred to as a 'sine tone' because the wave form, which may be observed by means of an oscilloscope, has the smooth undulation of a sine curve. Helmholtz's discovery thus opened up the possibility that one might mimic the sound of a piano by superimposing the requisite pure frequencies obtained from oscillators, or alternatively, and much more intriguingly, that one might compose entirely new timbres by creating combinations different from those emitted by any natural instrument. Such a technique would enable the composer to define an infinite variety of timbres with exactitude.

This was what Stockhausen began to attempt in two studies created at the Cologne studio in 1953–4, but his success was far from complete, for the pieces proved that the mechanisms of synthesizing and perceiving timbre were still improperly understood. Even so, the *Studien* are fascinating and beautiful; at the very least they demonstrated that the future of electronic music was to lie more with the creation of the new than with the *musique concrète* technique of readjusting the old.

Stockhausen next went on to tackle the problem of combining purely electronic sounds with natural ones, those of a boy's singing voice, and produced in his *Gesang der Jünglinge* (1955–6) what is perhaps the first piece of tape music to rise from the level of laboratory study to that of concert work. At one stroke he had shown that electronic music could take full possession of language, that the new medium could be made viable in the concert hall by having the audience surrounded by several banks of loudspeakers (the original version was for five tape tracks, later reduced to four) and that the antithesis between *Elektronische Musik* and *musique concrète* could be resolved.

Developments: the classic studio

Work in electronic music was now developing rapidly all over the globe, helped by the spread of the tape recorder. Cage's *Imaginary Landscape no. 5* (1951–2), using material from fifty-two gramophone records, was probably the first piece of tape music composed in America, to be followed swiftly by the work of Vladimir Ussachevsky and Otto Luening. Their endeavours stemmed from the gift of a tape recorder to Columbia University in 1951. Ussachevsky, who taught at the university, soon realized that the machine could be used creatively, and in 1952 he presented a demonstration of the possibilities. He was joined by Luening, who had been a pupil of Busoni, and the two began composing tape pieces, usually employing the sounds of musical instruments as sources. They gave their first concert at the Museum of Modern Art in New York on 28 October 1953, when the programme included Ussachevsky's *Sonic Contours*, created from piano recordings, and Luening's *Fantasy in Space*, taking flute sounds as raw material. By this time Louis and Bebe Barron had set up a private electronic music studio in New York, providing suitably strange soundtracks for such films as the science-fiction *Tempest* travesty *Forbidden Planet* (1956), and it was on their premises that Cage composed his *Imaginary Landscape no. 5* and also his *Williams Mix* (1952), a collage made up of all kinds of material, from purely electronic sounds to pre-existing music, from amplified 'small sounds' (Cage's own term for the barely audible) to city noises.

During the period from 1948 to 1954, therefore, the technical and aesthetic foundations of electronic music had been firmly established. The transformations made possible by the tape recorder and allied equipment – changes of speed, reversing, editing, superimposing, synthesizing new sounds – had quickly been discovered and put to use in a whole variety of ways. In particular, electronic means had opened up four new approaches to musical composition: using natural and man-made sounds (Schaeffer, Henry), altering the sounds of musical instruments (Schaeffer, Ussachevsky, Luening), creating new sound material (Eimert, Stockhausen) and constructing heterogeneous collages (Cage). Composers at this time were still using equipment which had not been designed specifically for creating music (in many cases the tools were testing devices), but the versatility of the new medium had been amply demonstrated: the era of the 'classic studio', as it has come to be called, had arrived.

Outside the main centres of Paris, Cologne and New York there now arose other studios for electronic music. In 1955 the Studio di Fonologia was founded at the Milan station of Radio Audizioni Italiane by the young composers Luciano Berio and Bruno Maderna (who had already, in 1952 in Bonn, produced the first work to bring together live and electronic resources, his *Musica su due dimensioni* for flute, percussion and tape). The Milan studio provided an alternative working-place to Paris and Cologne for members of the international avant-garde, avoiding the rivalry between *musique concrète* and *Elektronische Musik*. It was there that the Belgian composer Henri Pousseur created his *Scambi* (1957), which overcame the problem of the eternal sameness of music on tape by offering several different sequences of material, these to be joined or superimposed according to the composer's instructions. It was in Milan, too, that Cage composed another collage piece, *Fontana Mix* (1958), which is again indeterminate in that it consists only of vague prescriptions for the preparation of a tape which can be played either alone or simultaneously with other music by the composer.

Further electronic music studios were established in Tokyo (Japanese radio, 1956), Warsaw (Polish radio, 1957), Munich (Siemens company, 1957), Eindhoven (Philips company, 1957), London (BBC Radiophonic Workshop, 1958) and Stockholm (Swedish radio, 1958). The BBC studio concentrated on providing functional music for radio and television, but the others combined such work with pure composition. Varèse, for instance, worked at Eindhoven on his *Poème électronique*, conceived for playing over 350 loudspeakers in the pavilion which Le Corbusier had designed for Philips at the Brussels world exhibition of 1958. It is most unfortunate that the pavilion was demolished after the event, resulting in the loss not only of a striking edifice but also of the space for which Varèse's only composition for tape alone was intended, there to be experienced along with multifarious visual images projected on to the interior walls.

The original studios of Paris and Cologne were by no means dormant during this period of growth. In Paris, with the departure of Henry to found his own private studio in 1958, the Groupe de Musique Concrète was reorganized as the Groupe de Recherches Musicales, but the emphasis continued to be on the use of recorded sounds. The Paris studio also continued to produce composers specializing almost exclusively in electronic music, Schaeffer now being joined by such men as François Bayle and Luc Ferrari. Iannis Xenakis, who had worked with Le Corbusier on the Philips pavilion for Brussels, was exceptional in proving himself in both conventional and electronic fields, and also in bringing his architectural imagination to bear on musical composition. His tape compositions, among the strongest examples of Parisian *musique concrète*, include *Bohor* (1962), an enveloping environment of sounds emerging from eight tracks, all obtained from pieces of oriental jewellery and a Laotian wind instrument. Meanwhile the Cologne studio carried on the work of creating music by solely electronic means, the greatest work composed there during this period being Stockhausen's *Kontakte* for four-channel tape (1958–60), which generates a whole new world of sound from the simple basic material of electronic pulses.

By contrast with the situation in Europe, where electronic music studios were being set up principally by radio stations and industrial companies, the development of the medium in the USA depended on the initiatives of individual composers and universities. The efforts of Ussachevsky and Luening eventually led, in 1959, to the formal establishment of the Columbia–Princeton Electronic Music Center in New York, and there Varèse completed work on his *Déserts* tapes in 1961. Gordon Mumma and Robert Ashley founded the Cooperative Studio for Electronic Music at Ann

Arbor, Michigan, in 1958; Morton Subotnick and others established the San Francisco Tape Music Center in 1960; and various universities, notably the University of Illinois at Urbana, set up their own studios.

It was at Urbana that Lejaren Hiller and Leonard Isaacson created something of a stir when they brought out their *Illiac Suite* for string quartet (1955–6), the first musical work 'composed' by a computer. The piece was not, of course, a spontaneous display of creative imagination on the part of the machine; Hiller and Isaacson gave it a programme of detailed instructions, setting rules and outlining possibilities, and from this the computer created its print-out, to be converted into standard musical notation by the human collaborators. Xenakis used analogous techniques from the late fifties onwards, though the most powerful use of computers has been in the field of sound synthesis rather than compositional game-playing. But that had to wait another decade for its full refinement.

New tools: synthesizers

By the early sixties many composers and electronic technicians were concerning themselves with finding sound-generating means which might be more efficient and versatile than those offered by the classic studio. If a composer were to produce an interesting and ambitious tape piece with the techniques of the fifties he had to spend many hours in the studio, often working largely by trial and error with equipment which was never intended for musical composition. Stockhausen's *Gesang der Jünglinge*, for instance, took eighteen months to prepare; his *Kontakte* two years. More rapid methods of working could be envisaged only if there were to be an instrument specially designed for artistic work in the medium, an electronic music synthesizer.

The first such instrument, a gargantuan assembly not to be confused with the modern synthesizer, was the RCA Synthesizer constructed by Harry Olsen and Herbert Belar as an apparatus for the artificial creation of human speech. The unique Mark II version, which was acquired by the Columbia–Princeton Center at its inception in 1959, is capable of producing and altering a wide variety of sounds. Oscillators and noise generators provide the raw material which the composer, giving the synthesizer its instructions on a punched paper roll, can obtain at will with a high degree of control over pitch, volume, duration and timbre. The RCA Mark II Synthesizer is thus a kind of super-instrument, one which has an enormous range of instrumental 'voices' and a great capacity to transform sound supplied to it. It is, however, disposed in favour of the conventional equal-tempered twelve-note scale, and has found its most adept exponent in the serialist Milton Babbitt, who has used it in all his electronic works.

Though such fine compositions as Babbitt's *Ensembles for Synthesizer* (1962–4) and *Philomel* (1963) have been composed on it, the RCA Synthesizer was a cul-de-sac in the technological development of electronic music. An invention of wider significance came in 1964 when Robert Moog constructed the first sound devices responsive to control voltages, a voltage-control oscillator and a voltage-control amplifier. Previously it had been necessary for a composer to 'tune' his equipment by hand in order to obtain the desired pitch, volume or whatever. Moog's inventions, which made it possible for this to be done by electronic signals, increased the speed and precision with which sounds could be created and at the same time paved the way towards the construction of an instrument for sound synthesis. With the miniaturization of electronics which was taking place simultaneously, and with the evolution of 'modular' systems (providing different modules with different functions in sound generation and alteration, the modules to be linked in alternative ways), the synthesizer could be born. In 1966 synthesizers designed by Moog and by Donald Buchla became available commercially, and in 1968 the release of Walter Carlos's *Switched On Bach*, a record of music by Bach played on a Moog synthesizer, brought the innovation to worldwide public attention. The Moog and Buchla synthesizers were intended primarily for the creation of tape music: Carlos's arrangements, for instance, could not have been played in the concert hall, since the instrument could play only one melodic line at a time. However, Paul Ketoff's synket, constructed in 1965 for the Rome-based American composer John Eaton, was designed specifically for live performance, and polyphonic synthesizers were on the market before the end of the decade. It was not long before they began to appear on the concert platform, not least at rock performances.

Out of the studio: live electronic music

The synthesizer thus has a place not only in tape music but also in live electronic performance, though that art was developing fast before synthesizers appeared on the scene. Indeed, Respighi should perhaps be regarded as the pioneer here, since he asked for a gramophone recording of a nightingale in his orchestral *Pini di Roma* (1924). Cage, however, went very much further in his *Imaginary Landscapes nos.* 1–2, described above, and also in the fourth work from the same series (1951), which is scored for performers on twelve radio sets.

The use of the tape recorder as a concert instrument was initiated by Mauricio Kagel, an Argentinian composer living in Cologne, in his *Transición II* (1958–9). Two musicians operate on a piano – one in the conventional manner, the other playing directly on the strings and woodwork – and two others work tape recorders so that the work can unite its 'present' of live sound with its 'future' of pre-recorded material from later on and its 'past' of recordings made earlier in the performance. Stockhausen's *Solo* (1965–6) has a single performer generate a polyphonic web of novelty and reminiscence by means of a tape recorder with movable heads, these allowing defined variations in the delay between recording and playback. Another feature of tape recording, the accumulation of feedback sounds within the open cycle of playback and re-recording, was exploited by Alvin Lucier in his *I am sitting in a room* (1970), where a spoken sentence is progressively obliterated by the growing strength of feedback sounds from the acoustic environment.

These works by Kagel, Stockhausen and Lucier virtually exhaust the possibilities of the tape recorder in live performance; a great deal more can be done with microphones, amplifiers and electronic modulators. The first example of live electronic music in the generally accepted sense was probably Cage's *Cartridge Music* (1960), an indeterminate score for several performers applying gramophone cartridges and contact microphones to various objects. This was followed by such works as *Variations IV* (1963) 'for any number of players, any sounds or combinations of sounds produced by any means, with or without other activities', the recordings of which present a pot-pourri of sounds and music new and old.

Stockhausen's live electronic music, always very much more organized than Cage's, began with his *Mikrophonie I* (1964), which requires six musicians to generate, pick up and project the wealth of sounds that can be drawn from a large tam-tam (square-rimmed gong). In his *Mixtur* (also 1964) he has the sounds of an orchestra transformed by means of ring modulators, which create an effect somewhat like that obtained when a radio is slightly mistuned. The result is often harsh in quality, but the ring modulator can be a powerful device for creating new sound relationships and new harmonies, as it is in *Mixtur* as well as in Stockhausen's later *Mikrophonie II* for choir, Hammond organ, electronics and tapes (1965) and *Mantra* for two pianos and electronics (1970). The use of the same apparatus in tape music, to achieve what Stockhausen terms the 'intermodulation' of different musical materials with each other, is well demonstrated in his *Telemusik* (1966), which brings together recordings of ethnic music from every continent to make a 'music of the whole world'.

In the sphere of live electronic music most was being achieved by small ensembles, whether rock bands or groups of avant-garde composers and performers. From the late sixties onwards such rock musicians as the Beatles, Frank Zappa and Pink Floyd were making use of live electronic techniques, often influenced by Stockhausen's work with his own ensemble in such compositions as *Kurzwellen* (1968). Here several performers on electronic or amplified instruments are required to respond to each other and to what they hear from shortwave radios. The score remains open to this foreign and unpredictable material, including no standard musical notation but instead detailing how the musicians should react and interact. *Kurzwellen* is thus well adapted to a medium in which sounds cannot easily be prescribed with complete accuracy, but in which individual performers have an enlarged capacity to mimic or blend with an alien sound.

Any performance by a live electronic ensemble is bound to be at least in part improvisatory, and some have chosen to concentrate on that approach: AMM, a London group active in the late sixties, was one such. Others have established distinctive styles in 'group compositions', as Musica Elettronica Viva, an ensemble of American musicians working in Rome during the late sixties, did in their *Spacecraft*. Still others, like Stockhausen's group, have been dominated by the personality of a single composer, or else, like the American Sonic Arts Union, worked on compositions by individual members.

Live electronic works for larger forces, like Stockhausen's *Mixtur*, have remained few, partly because of the reluctance of orchestral musicians to work with equipment for which usually their training has provided no preparation. There was a notorious demonstration of that in 1962, when members of the New York Philharmonic Orchestra disrupted the electronic apparatus required for them to play Cage's *Atlas eclipticalis*, and Stockhausen met with an unsympathetic response when, in 1970, he tried to engage the BBC Symphony Orchestra in 'intuitive' electronic music-making. Work of this kind, performed without a score but through a meditative response to a text of the composer's, has proved much easier to achieve with small groups.

But live electronic music has not thereby been limited to a modest scale, for the medium lends itself well to performance in spectacular locations, places where the visual environment can match the strangeness and often the grandeur of the sounds. Stockhausen has performed with his ensemble in a Lebanese cavern and in a spherical auditorium specially designed for him at Expo 70 in Osaka, while his *Sternklang* (1971) was conceived for several live electronic ensembles playing in a public park under a starlit sky. Unusual venues have also been favoured by Xenakis for his tape music: his *Persepolis* (1971) was created for the ruins of the ancient Persian city, and he has also composed works of electronic sound and laser light for a Roman bath-house and a city square in Paris.

Newer developments: computer sound, minimalism

The evolution of live electronic music brought a change of emphasis and, to some degree, a neglect of the electronic music studio: Stockhausen, for instance, has composed no new work for tape alone since his *Hymnen* (1966–7). Other composers during the late sixties, however, found the potential of tape music greatly expanded thanks to advances in sound synthesis by computer. The leading investigator in this field has been the American scientist Max Mathews, who in 1958, at the Bell Telephone Laboratories in New Jersey, started work on devising computer programs which would enable composers to stipulate minute details of the sounds they wished to create, giving precise instructions for every element of pitch, duration, timbre and so on. By 1964 such programs were available, and by the end of the decade they had been used in sound synthesis by several composers, notably Gottfried Michael Koenig in Utrecht and James K. Randall and Charles Dodge at the universities of Princeton and Columbia.

Computer sound synthesis has the advantages that the computer, unlike most synthesizers, can deal with any number of musical lines at a time, that it obviates the need for any manual control and so makes possible a greater rhythmic precision, and that details of a composition can readily be altered (by attention to the program) while the rest remains intact. It is perhaps through the use of computers in sound generation, which is still an area of active research, that the great dream of electronic music – the realization of musical conceptions without any limits other than those of the imagination – will at last become a possibility.

For some musicians, however, computer sound synthesis does not offer so utopian a prospect, while live electronic music appears too uncontrolled a medium. The revived interest in consonant harmony and a slow rate of change, as exhibited in the 'minimalist' music of such American composers as LaMonte Young, Terry Riley, Steve Reich and Philip Glass since the late sixties, has often gone together with the use of electronic instruments of more conventional type, especially electric organs and pianos. In works like Riley's *A Rainbow in Curved Air* (1969) or Reich's *Four Organs* (1970) the electronic element is diminished in importance, though it may suggest a kinship with contemporary rock music; the main musical interest is in the exact and obsessive patterning which instruments without moving parts can most readily achieve.

By the time of the centenary of Edison's phonograph in 1977, therefore, electronic music had become a field of diverse endeavour, different composers working with electronic musical instruments, classic tape techniques, live electronics, computers and synthesizers. And in that same year of 1977 wide-ranging research into music and technology was inaugurated under the direction of Pierre Boulez at the Institut de Recherche et Coordination Acousti-que/Musique in Paris. It may well be that the work of IRCAM will make a definitive contribution to the further development of electronic music, which seems most likely to proceed on the fronts of computer sound synthesis, the building of new performance instruments, the integration of musical with visual presentation on videotape and the application of live electronics with greater sophistication. But it is hazardous to prophesy at this stage: the past of electronic music suggests only that its future will be unpredictable.

I.3 Approach

Before various aspects of electronic music are examined in more detail it may be useful to suggest possible avenues of approach, even though the wide range of creative work in the medium makes it difficult to generalize.

In the first place it is worth remembering that electronic music is a new art, much newer than film as an effective medium, and that it is still in a state of rapid development. The resources available to the first composers of tape music, at the beginning of the fifties, seem primitive indeed when compared with the elaborate instrumentation and the advanced technical knowledge which composers now have at their disposal. And since electronic music is unusually dependent on the means accessible at the time – tape pieces are created once and for all, and even live electronic works have to be geared to the equipment of the day – it follows that a certain historical awareness is necessary in approaching electronic compositions. Any judgment must take into account the efficiency and imagination with which the composer has used what was at hand, in terms both of apparatus and of theoretical knowledge concerning the composition and perception of sound.

To take an example from a field which may be more familiar, it will probably help one's appreciation of piano music during the period from Mozart to Liszt if one knows something of the changes that were taking place in instrument design. The case for such background knowledge is still greater in electronic music, since the evolution has been so much faster and more far-reaching. Even so, it would be wrong to infer that only an electronics engineer can gain an informed understanding of electronic music. The broad outlines are enough, for, to take Schoenberg's words from a different context, the listener is concerned primarily with 'what it is', not 'how it is made'.

The case is, of course, very different for the composer. He needs to be thoroughly familiar with electronic equipment before he can use it constructively, and yet his education and experience will not, most probably, have fitted him for work in the new medium. Not only that, electronic composition demands quite new modes of thought. As Boulez wrote after his first venture into the electronic studio, 'the electronic means themselves will initially cause the composer to be confused; he will be unable to reconcile them with his traditional ideas of sound ... everything which was limited becomes unlimited; everything which was "imponderable" can now be subjected to precise measurement'. Furthermore, if tape music is in question, the composer finds himself for the first time in the position of unique executant: the work is fixed for all time, and fixed by him.

This fixedness of tape music causes diverse problems. There is no opportunity for different performances to provide alternative views, and so, unless the composer is content for his work to be disposable, he must make something which will hold interest through repeated identical hearings (though perhaps this is not so acute a limitation when recordings provide so much of our musical experience). Some composers have attempted to loosen the tape medium, by making sequences which can be differently arranged, as in Pousseur's *Scambi* (1957) and Boucourechliev's *Texte II* (1959), or else by publishing a work in the form of instructions, as Koenig did in his *Essay* (1957–8). But such efforts do not circumvent the problem of there being no interpreter to add the 'imponderable' nuances of musical performance, a disability which accounts for the rhythmic characterlessness of much tape music. It is still the composer's responsibility to give his music all its subtlety of gesture and of sound.

The creation of new sounds is very often important in both tape pieces and live electronic music, and so the quality of sound reproduction can become a limiting factor in the appreciation of the music. Poor reproduction of vocal or instrumental music can diminish the experience, but rarely to the extent that the sounds become unrecognizable: we can still distinguish and savour a flute, for instance, because we have learned to let memory add to whatever distorted picture we hear from a recording, just as we have learned to hear familiar voices in the inferior imitations which

25

emerge from a telephone. When the sounds are completely new, however, there can be no help from the memory. It follows that an electronic work, though designed for artificial means of reproduction, may paradoxically lose more when played through a low-fidelity sound system than will a work for conventional forces, and this is something often overlooked when electronic music is performed in the concert hall.

Creating new sounds is sometimes regarded as an ignoble aim in music, and yet one has only to compare Beethoven's orchestration with that of Haydn, for example, to convince oneself that innovation in this domain can be an essential part of a composer's thinking. So it is in electronic music, over a vaster plane and therefore to a greater extent. And yet the expanded universe of electronic sound has encouraged many composers to a lack of discretion and discernment, with the result that one may easily form the impression that the electronic sound world is more limited than the orchestral, that electronic pieces tend to sound the same. Many of the greatest works in the medium, however, stand out for their originality of sound, and for the finesse with which their sounds are composed. It becomes apparent that this is no easy matter, but that skill and imagination are needed to make sounds which retain their sense of wonder.

Sounds, and not notes, are very often definitively the material in a medium which bypasses the notated score. There are fine electronic works that are restricted to the tempered chromatic scale with which we are familiar, Babbitt's *Ensembles for Synthesizer* for one, but more often the composer will take advantage of the liberation from pitch conventions which electronic music affords. Frequently this means that the resulting work will not allow pitch the primacy it holds in most music for traditional resources. We may have to look elsewhere for a sense of order, and so we need to be attentive to the whole quality of the sound. Where Bach, for example, uses sounds principally as vehicles of pitch and rhythm, so that his music can be arranged (even for electronic sound) without great loss, an electronic composer may be concerned most of all with timbre.

Yet music is not made with sounds alone but with sounds in context. Exactly how the sounds in an electronic work will be related is, of course, something that will vary greatly from one composition to another. They may not be related at all, though in that case we may well regard the piece as a negligible achievement. If there is a relation, then it may be at the level of a traditional compositional technique, such as the serial method used by Babbitt in his tape compositions as in those for conventional forces: here the particular value of the electronic medium, as far as the composer is concerned, lies in the ease with which quantities, particularly rhythmic quantities, can be determined, and in the guarantee of a perfect performance. In other cases coherence may be established in the repertory of sounds, perhaps by restricting the music to those which can be obtained from a single instrument or electronic source; this is the case, for example, in many early pieces of *musique concrète* and also in Stockhausen's live electronic *Mikrophonie I*. Then again, the composer may link sounds by some external reference. Ligeti's *Artikulation* is a simple instance of this, concerning itself with sounds and patterns which, though entirely synthetic, cry out to be heard as substitute human speech.

More generally, the electronic medium has stimulated composers to consider music as process rather than form, and so to create, in many cases, works in perpetual evolution. Electronic means make it possible to generate sounds of long duration and, more importantly, gradual change, so that an electronic work, whether for tape or live resources, can mirror in its progress the techniques of timbre composition and transformation used in its creation. Stockhausen's works provide abundant examples of this approach, which may result in a kind of aural drama conducted by the sounds themselves (and not to be confused with the banal use of sounds as sound effects in much inferior electronic music). The listener is obliged to suspend expectations and to follow, in every moment, the path unfolded by the music. And though there may be no room for the listener's unconscious prediction, electronic music can still hold powerful surprises. It is true that the medium makes it only too easy to indulge in trick effects: bizarre juxtapositions of unrelated ideas, sudden shifts from the familiar to the unfamiliar, gradual disruptions of everyday sounds. Yet these devices can also, in the hands of a sensitive musician, give rise to that wonder which is not an insignificant part of our experience of electronic music. The wonder of new discovery, of having one's preconceptions overturned, is part of the excitement of the art.

Electronic music also has, apart from the resources of sound which have been mentioned, a new ability to deal with the extramusical world. The added dimension of language has been available to musicians since the birth of the art, but electronic music is unprecedented in its capacity to draw directly from mundane experience by means of recordings. An orchestral work can only suggest the world outside, by means, for example, of trumpet fanfares for a military milieu, whereas an electronic piece can point such references with much greater precision and over a much wider range: Luigi Nono's *La fabbrica illuminata*, for soprano and tape, can make clear statements about industrial life by immersing itself in the factory sound world. It is necessary for the listener, therefore, to be alive not only to internal, purely musical meanings but also to immediate references extending into every aspect of human existence; and he may well find that some of the most powerful tape pieces have a depth of significance on both counts.

If this makes electronic music a potentially realist art, one should note also its propensity for the surreal. We hear music on tape without being able to associate the sounds with any instrument, and even in live electronic music the aural results may well seem to be out of all proportion to the activity observed: when a violinist reaches into the upper register, or when a pianist strives for maximum volume, the strain is evident in the way he comports himself (and we may even feel that strain in a recording), but the technique of electronic instruments involves no such relationship between sound and gesture. Sound seems to blossom independently of any sounding body or human action, and again our reaction may be one of wonder, or disquiet. In particular, the distortion of vocal or instrumental sound immediately places it in some territory between the known and the unknown, so that electronic music can readily speak in the language of dreams and nightmares, or, more rarely, in that of religious experience.

On the other hand the medium is, by its very nature, peculiarly well adapted to concern itself with the worldly condition of man faced by technology. Nor need this be a cause for anxiety. Just as we admire a violinist's ability to produce something beautiful from the intractable materials of hair, metal and wood, so we may take pleasure when an electronic composer creates beauty and order, as so many have done, from a benign interaction with magnetic tapes and electrical circuits; and we may draw a warning where we find the relationship to be less than equal. Far from being 'inhuman' or 'robotic', as was often charged in the early days, electronic music is thus a profoundly human art. It is also one that seems peculiarly appropriate at a time when electronic means, the radio and the gramophone, are the principal sources of musical experience for the vast majority of people in technologically developed countries. We may even reflect, with Herbert Eimert, 'whether perhaps it is not the symphony recorded on tape or disc that is the synthetic, and electronic music the genuine article'.

II   The electronic repertory

The following eight chapters deal with particular facets of electronic music and consider some of the outstanding contributions to the medium. The categorization is inevitably arbitrary to some degree, but not unhelpful if it gives some impression of the main technical and aesthetic directions. Almost all of the works mentioned have been commercially recorded.

II.1   Out of the known

Electronic music, if we date its origins from Pierre Schaeffer's first essays in *musique concrète*, emerged out of the known world of sounds, and the use of natural sources, often transformed in some manner, has remained a central technique in tape music of all kinds. But Schaeffer's first study, the *Etude aux chemins de fer*, which he created in May 1948 from recordings of locomotives of rolling stock, not only initiated a genre; it also brought the composer up against one of the main difficulties of the medium. If the sounds remain recognizable, then they are evocative symbols rather than, as Schaeffer wished, 'sound objects' freed from their associations in the real world. To depend on those associations would be, in Schaeffer's terms, to create not music but literature: the work becomes a drama of sound effects rather than a musical composition of rhythms and timbres.

The means which Schaeffer discovered to produce genuine 'sound objects' – techniques of speed and direction change, cutting and superimposition – have been mentioned in chapter I.2. His methods opened up a whole new range of raw material for musical composition, but they provided no suggestions as to how such material might be used. Only in his theoretical writings did Schaeffer consider the new structural processes, including serial manipulation, to which recorded sound might be subjected; in his early studies he remained content with building simple rhythmic patterns and straightforward sectional forms, and his later attempts to catalogue 'sound objects' led him to an unproductive concentration on the definition of material rather than its creative development.

It remained for other composers, notably Pierre Boulez, to show how a serial approach to *musique concrète* could result in the accommodation of new sounds within new forms. Boulez's two tape *Etudes* (1952), dating from the same period as his investigation of total serialism in the first book of *Structures* for two pianos, have an importance beyond their modest duration in that they eschew both established formal principles and the evocative allure of sound trickery. The first study is constructed entirely from transformations of a single sound on the zanzi (an exotic percussion instrument), and so interest is focused squarely on the capacity of the medium to modify. There is no juxtaposition, only composition, and the piece becomes an essay in the variation of rhythm and sound quality.

Such abstraction was, however, to remain rare in electronic music based on recordings of natural sounds. More commonly composers have sought to show what a wealth of material can be generated from simple sources, to shock with the unexpected, and very often to capitalize on the expressive potency of strange sounds and surprising progressions. Pierre Henry, the most inventive and certainly the most prolific composer to have served an apprenticeship in the Paris studio, has frequently worked in this way. The fifteen short pieces of his *Le microphone bien tempéré* (1950–51) show the facility with which he quickly learned to master the time-consuming techniques of creating music from disc recordings; he also collaborated with Schaeffer on the *Symphonie pour un homme seul* (1949–50), which uses a wide variety of sounds – vocal, instrumental and orchestral, as well as many from household objects – as the basis of eleven short movements diverse in character, by turn erotic, whimsical or menacing.

In its illustrative nature and expressive appeal, recognized when Maurice Béjart chose to choreograph it in 1955, the *Symphonie* set the style for Henry's later music, including several other works for Béjart: *Orphée* (1958), *Le voyage* (1961–2), *La reine verte* (1963), *Messe pour le temps présent* (1967) and *Mouvement-rythme-étude*

(1970, choreographed as *Nijinsky, clown de Dieu*) among others. Most of Henry's important works are long by comparison with other tape compositions, in many cases filling a long-playing record, and often they present themselves ambitiously as vehicles of mystical experience. *Le voyage*, a journey into the after-life based on the Tibetan Book of the Dead, is typical of Henry's aesthetic approach and of the awe-inspiring skill with which he wields sound on tape. The work is, in fact, composed wholly from synthetic material, even though there are sounds which suggest breathing, for example. However, Henry's approach has been conditioned by the methods of *musique concrète*, and his achievements have influenced a great many other composers in that medium.

The work of the Turkish–American composer Ilhan Mimaroglu can be compared with that of Henry in both method and style. Like Henry, Mimaroglu is a composer exclusively of electronic music and has concentrated on the resources of the classic studio; both composers create music which is direct in its imagery. Examples of Mimaroglu's *musique concrète* include *Bowery Bum* (1964), made from the sounds of a rubber band, and *Wings of the Delirious Demon* (1969), where a clarinet is the unique source of material, its voice sometimes bizarrely altered by ring modulation or other means. This latter work, beginning in ominous darkness, rising to great battles of sound and concluding with a lament, well demonstrates the dramatic force of Mimaroglu's longer soundscapes.

His shorter pieces, like the set of twelve Preludes (1966–7), tend to be more static and to dwell on a confined area of sound material, such as the pretty celesta–harpsichord combination of Prelude no. 8 or the studio-extended guitar of no. 6. He has, again like Henry, used pure electronic synthesis, for example in *Agony* (1965), but again the intention is primarily descriptive or pictorial. Not surprisingly, the ideas for his pieces have sometimes come from the work of painters: Dubuffet in *Bowery Bum*, Arshile Gorky in *Agony* and Pollock in what the composer aptly calls the 'drips and smears' of *White Cockatoo* (1966).

However, the variety of poetic electronic music favoured by Henry and Mimaroglu is best exemplified not by any of their works but by Varèse's *Poème électronique* (1957–8). Though it lasts for only eight minutes this work is among the small number of masterpieces of tape music, having a strength of utterance which makes most other *musique concrète* appear trivial or overweening. Great blocks of sound, intricate rhythmic counterpoints and electronically generated melodies are among the raw materials, along with specific references to earlier works by the composer, these references seeming to assert a claim for the work as the crown of his career in tirelessly seeking new sounds and combinations. It is at the same time a powerfully expressive piece, 'a protest against inquisition in every form' as Varèse called it, with a solo soprano voice entering in imprecation close to the end, a human being at the centre of the strange and seemingly malevolent world the music conjures.

Varèse's great achievement in the *Poème électronique* was to create a sound drama whose imagery is not, as in much *musique concrète*, trivial or cheap. The tolling bells, the disembodied voices and the macabre stuttering organ all have an immediate evocative power, but the constant drive of the imaginative momentum keeps all in check. Of the many fragments only a rising three-note figure, recalling similar gestures in Varèse's other works, is allowed to recur and so to articulate the development. And yet, though the piece ranges so widely and swiftly, every event appears to have been chosen and placed with great care, the composer attentive not only to its expressive effect but also to its properties of rhythm, colour and pitch. This is indeed 'organized sound', to use Varèse's own term, and not just a collage.

Iannis Xenakis, who as Le Corbusier's assistant had contact with Varèse during the composition of the *Poème électronique*, has used *musique concrète* techniques rather differently in his own tape works. Like his compositions for conventional media, these are most often concerned with mass effects; the mathematics of probability, sometimes invoked with the aid of a computer, generally play a part in the calculation of dense textures and slow transformations. *Concret PH* (1958), composed like the *Poème électronique* for the Philips pavilion at the Brussels exhibition, is typical: the piece is created from, and sounds like, the crackling of burning charcoal, though the composer would see his material as building great curved sweeps, or 'hyperbolic paraboloids' (hence the title). Setting aside *Bohor* (1962), another monolithic sound sculpture but on a massive scale, Xenakis's most subtle electronic music is to be found in his *Orient-occident* (1959–60), where his careful relation of adjacent sounds suggests the influence of Schaeffer's contemporary *Etude aux objets*. Xenakis excels Schaeffer, however, in the boldness with which he uses the medium, most effectively in the grand climax of this work and in the swirling glissandos at a similar point in the more openly dramatic *Diamorphoses* (1957).

Xenakis's works, like the otherwise very different studies of Boulez, exemplify the use of *musique concrète* to abstract ends: the origins of the sounds are not that important, and the composer does not attempt to invest them with metaphysical significance. Such abstraction may be more easily achieved if the composer works with sounds which already are exclusively musical in their associations: the sounds, that is, of conventional instruments. This was the method adopted by Luening and Ussachevsky in their first experiments of 1951–2, Luening working with the flute and Ussachevsky with the piano. Strangely enough, Schaeffer had used similar instruments in his two *Etudes au piano* (1948) and *Variations sur une flûte mexicaine* (1949).

The application of the usual *musique concrète* transformations enabled all three composers to create sounds beyond the expected, whether bizarre timbres (Schaeffer's *Etude au piano I*), polyphonies obtained by mixing several different recordings (Ussachevsky's *Sonic Contours*), or notes below the normal range of the instrument (Luening's *Low Speed*). There are, however, marked aesthetic differences between the French and American works. Schaeffer, like the Parisian composers who followed him in using instrumental sounds, appears fascinated by the surreal, disturbing effects of distortion. In the pieces by Luening and Ussachevsky, on the other hand, the joy in creating atmospheric strokes goes along with an almost boyish enthusiasm in discovering the potentialities of a new medium, and this spirit of adventure persists in such later works as Ussachevsky's *Of Wood and Brass* (1965). Here the sounds are all obtained literally from wood (xylophone) and brass (trumpet, trombone and Korean gong), but only rarely can the sources be distinguished, since Ussachevsky edits much more freely than in his earlier music and also uses electronic modulation.

The Swedish composer Bengt Hambraeus has also used instrumental sounds in tape music, but without such drastic revisions of timbre. His *Tetragon* (1965) is 'scored' for an ensemble of flute, trumpet, voice, percussion, harpsichord, clavichord and large organ, a grouping which would be unlikely to prove effective in the concert hall but which can be balanced without difficulty in the studio. Hambraeus uses electronic techniques to generate, for example, swooping glissandos in his organ material or, at the impressive opening of the work, echoing trumpet fanfares from all four channels, but often the recording is natural, the studio being employed only to create complex counterpoints of unrelated musical streams or to bring various groups and instruments into and out of focus.

With the arrival of computer sound synthesis in the mid-sixties the creation of *musique concrète* became very much simpler, though many composers, including Mimaroglu and the group working at the Paris studio, have continued to prefer classic studio techniques. A computer allows the composer to store his raw material in its memory and then to call out sounds at will, without having to go through tedious processes of cutting and splicing tape. Moreover, the re-synthesis of sounds can be so affected as to alter the pitches and durations of the original recordings, and so transformations too can be carried out automatically. These techniques have been most used with recordings of the human voice, but Harrison Birtwistle's *Chronometer* (1971) provides an example of their application to other materials and indicates the refinement of *musique concrète* thus made possible.

Birtwistle here uses recordings of clock mechanisms, the whole piece being a controlled collage of ticking timepieces, cast in a veil caused by the imperfection of the computer re-synthesis. The everyday associations of the material, with irrevocably passing time, are entirely at one with the work's musical purpose. Sometimes sounding like a vast percussion ensemble, the clocks unswervingly continue in a work which is given shape by varieties of texture and by the occasional bell stroke, a work which might well serve to justify Stravinsky's definition of music as 'establishing an order in things, including, and particularly, the coordination between *man* and *time*'. Scarcely less remarkable, and very rare in works using known sounds, is Birtwistle's achievement in creating a composition in which, to return to Schaeffer's terms, music is not compromised by literature.

II.2 The electronic voice

Electronic music which uses one particular range of known sounds, those of the human voice, demands separate treatment, since the possibilities here are rich and unusual. In most western music the involvement of the voice has meant also the involvement of words, with the almost inevitable result of an antagonism between music and text, both battling for the centre of attention; works such as Delibes' *Lakmé* or Debussy's *Sirènes* provide rare examples of textless singing, or vocalise, used for special dramatic or poetic effect. Under less exceptional circumstances, to have a singer mouthing unintelligible syllables would be to invite the danger of absurdity. However, when the voice appears on tape this restriction is lifted, the unseen singer no longer needing to behave with rational decorum. Henry's *Vocalise* (1952), which is constructed entirely from the sound 'ah', shows indeed that electronic vocalise can be powerfully atmospheric, and this discovery, strangely enough, has liberated composers not only to develop the field opened by Henry but also to pursue textless utterance in works for live performance. It is arguable that Berio's *Sequenza III* for solo voice (1965) would not have been possible if its meaningless sounds had not been legitimized by earlier electronic pieces, notably those of Berio himself.

In the field of vocal music with language, electronic music has been no less important in establishing new possibilities. An electronic work can resolve, as no work for conventional forces can, the antagonism between music and text, since the words themselves can become purely musical material. Techniques of distortion, when applied to sung or spoken language, can place the meaning in doubt, so that the sound of the words is made more important than their sense; moreover, the all-encompassing freedom of the electronic medium gives the composer scope to make smooth connections between vocal and non-vocal material, abolishing the dichotomy between voice and accompaniment. Such possibilities, taking composers close to the interests of sound poets, have led Stockhausen, Berio and others to concern themselves directly with the functional and phonetic structures of language, and so to approach texts, whether in electronic or in live compositions, with a more analytic understanding.

Stockhausen's *Gesang der Jünglinge* on multi-track tape (1955–6) was the first work to explore a mediation between music and language, and it remains the most abundantly successful composition of its kind. The text is taken from the *Benedicite* ('O all ye works of the Lord, bless ye the Lord . . .'), which appears in the Apocryphal chapters of Daniel as the canticle sung by the three young Jews consigned to a furnace by Nebuchadnezzar: hence the title of 'Song of the Young Men'. But Stockhausen does not use his extract as a fixed object to be set; instead he works with it freely, so that isolated words and phonemes appear more frequently than do coherent phrases, and, moreover, the word order is disrupted. Since the text can be taken as familiar, at least to a German-speaking audience, the work can play with different levels of verbal communication, from direct statement through various degrees of scrambling to total confusion. Thus Stockhausen introduces a quite new way of handling language which has been enormously influential, by no means only in electronic music, and which must count among his most powerful contributions to compositional technique.

Gesang is not, however, a composition of verbal fragments alone. The words, sung by a boy treble, are combined with electronically generated sounds which provide not an accompaniment but a parallel dimension enmeshed with the voice. By using standard studio methods in his treatment of the voice – excerpting brief moments, constructing a 'chorus' by superimposing several recordings, playing a recording in reverse – Stockhausen is able to make us perceive vocal utterance as pure sound. And by creating artificial sounds which approach vowels and consonants he can make the electronic material seem sometimes like garbled language. The work thus presents a fully integrated continuum from textual phrases which can readily be understood to completely meaningless electronic sounds, and so for the first time linguistic sense is absorbed into a musical work, a work which stands among the most remarkable examples of creative virtuosity in the classic studio.

One important feature of the piece, though perhaps a side-effect of the composer's plan, is the highly dramatic character of the disembodied voice. Whether the work is heard from a single pair of loudspeakers or, as Stockhausen originally intended, from several banks surrounding the audience, the boy's voice is released from association with the singer. It breaks all the rules of vocal behaviour – in disintegrating its text, sounding from more than one place at once and rapidly shifting position – and so takes on a quite unaccustomed power as pure song.

The theatrical potential of the electronic voice is used in a very different manner by Berio in his *Thema – omaggio a Joyce* (1958) and *Visage* (1961), both of which ask to be heard as psychological documents. In *Thema* the sole sound material is a recitation of a passage from *Ulysses* by a female voice. First the extract is heard complete; then it is electronically manipulated in such a way that intelligible phrases emerge occasionally from a stream of varied distortions. Inevitably one is tempted to interpret the breakdown of the text as a metaphor of mental disintegration, and this temptation to interpret the sounds as drama becomes still stronger in *Visage*.

Here Berio combines the voice of Cathy Berberian with electronic sounds, and there are places, as in Stockhausen's *Gesang*, where the two sources mimic each other and are confused. In *Visage*, however, the voice is a character, heard in a natural recording almost throughout the work. The accent is on non-verbal communication: the voice laughs, sobs, moans, gabbles in nonsense language and only twice struggles to enunciate a comprehensible word, 'parole' (words). Thanks to the intimacy of the electronic medium, which places such works as *Visage* in the theatre of the mind, one has the feeling that one is observing a woman in the emotional turmoil of anguish, fear, hysteria and sexual arousal.

Straight recording of the voice is also used in Henri Pousseur's tape works *Jeu de miroirs de Votre Faust* (1966) and *Trois visages de Liège* (1961). The former is one of several reflections by the composer on his opera *Votre Faust*: this one takes a performance of *Miroir de Votre Faust*, for piano with soprano, as its basis, adding spoken litanies from the librettist Michel Butor and fragments of sung material, all to make an 'intimate diary' of the opera's main personage. As in much of Pousseur's music, the density of allusion, both musical and linguistic, creates a dreamlike ambience. The *Trois visages de Liège*, however, are more mundane, tied to little poems which speak of the Belgian city's gay atmosphere and its industrial life. Sometimes recalling Stockhausen's *Gesang* and recent *Kontakte*, the work reveals an indebtedness felt not only by

Pousseur but also by many other European composers during the fifties and early sixties.

Luigi Nono was, like Pousseur, closely associated with Stockhausen at the beginning of his career, but his music, which includes several electronic works involving the human voice, is utterly distinctive, impelled by his passionate adherence to the cause of socialism. The unique capacity of the electronic medium to enter the sound world of heavy industry – already demonstrated in such works as Pousseur's *Trois visages de Liège* and Varèse's *Déserts* – is of obvious attraction to a composer wishing to deal with political reality, and in *La fabbrica illuminata* (1964) Nono creates a rough, aggressive tape from sounds gathered in an Italian factory, together with electronically treated choral singing. All this is overlaid by a live or recorded soprano singing a lyrical protest against the inhuman existence forced upon industrial labour, a protest which recalls the composer's dictum that the human voice can be 'a symbol of life, of love, and of freedom from all new forms of oppression and neo-Nazi torture'.

Nono's effects are often broad and direct, sometimes coarse, but he refuses to be led by his socialist convictions to create music which is banal. The strident and sombre textures of his tape piece *Ricorda cosa ti hanno fatto in Auschwitz* (1966) offer a memorial which is fiercely expressive and yet dignified by its honesty; no words could be sufficient to communicate the horror, and so Nono composes his frozen scream from the wailing of high soprano and children's chorus, and from purely electronic sounds. His later works for combinations of voices, instruments and tape, including *Contrappunto dialettico alla mente* (1967–8), *Non consumiamo Marx* (1969) and *Y entonces comprendio* (1969–70), are among the most forceful examples of committed music to have come out of the period around 1968. Nor does Nono fail to recognize that he is addressing a complex situation, even if these works bear witness in the first place to his simple humanity. *Y entonces comprendio*, for example, is a fervent lament for fallen heroes of the Cuban revolution and also a banner of encouragement for those that follow; the piece is essentially a spare interplay of recorded female voices which seem to reach out from the loudspeakers, but at the end it is brought squarely into the real world with live choral participation, the voice of Castro and recordings from street demonstrations. For Nono the electronic voice is the most urgent medium for musical manifestos in an age of mass communications.

It is a rather different electronic voice which speaks to us from the computer vocal works of Charles Dodge, who has led the way in developing the musical possibilities of computer speech synthesis. His technique depends on the computer's ability to analyse speech submitted to it and then to use this analysis in the creation of speech sounds, on to which the composer can impose new pitches, timbres and durations. *In Celebration* (1975) effectively shows the possibilities: the computer is able to provide real speech melodies, so that music enters directly into language as it does in Stockhausen's *Gesang der Jünglinge*, with which *In Celebration* can be compared in the variety of its vocal textures (including close harmony redolent of the Beach Boys). Dodge also uses computer speech synthesis in *The Story of our Lives* (1974), a miniature 'opera' for one male and one female character, together with a 'book' which talks through strange glistening streams of glissandos. Re-creation of speech by computer has not yet been perfected – Dodge's characters sound irredeemably catarrhal – but it would seem to hold immense promise as a technique enabling composers to exert exact control over verbal material.

Like the Dodge piece just described, Babbitt's *Philomel* (1963) is a dramatic scene, set at the instant when the tongueless Philomel of Ovid's story undergoes metamorphosis into a nightingale. Since the work calls for a live soprano as well as the recorded soprano on tape, the transformation can be accomplished, as it were, through the mirror of the loudspeakers, the soloist seeming to oscillate between human being (live singer) and pure voice (recording). At the same time, the dense interweaving of electronically synthesized polyphony, very much characteristic of Babbitt's tape music, gives the work a firm musical continuity and also makes a poetic contribution in suggesting the nocturnal forest through which Philomel runs. The work is rare and valuable in so combining structural rigour with direct effectiveness, achieving something Babbitt had missed in his *Vision and Prayer*, where an expressionist vocal treatment of Dylan Thomas's images of physical and spiritual birth is set against an oddly nonchalant accompaniment.

Two works by Kenneth Gaburo, *Antiphony III* (1962) and *Antiphony IV* (1967), show the medium of voices with tape being used in a manner which invites comparison with Stockhausen or Berio rather than with the composer's compatriot Babbitt. Both pieces are concerned with antiphony in a variety of senses, most particularly with antiphonies between live and electronic resources and between, once more, music and language. *Antiphony III*, the longer and simpler composition, uses chorus and tape in a tapestry of mutual imitation, whereas *Antiphony IV* uses voices, instruments and tape in dissecting a short poem into detached phonemes, which may be separated by or superimposed upon the purely musical sounds of instruments and electronics. In both pieces, however, the effect is the same: the non-verbal elements of the music are drawn into coherent patterns by the listener's determination to make the vocal events congeal into a poem.

There remains for consideration the use of electronics to transform vocal tone in live performance, so far a curiously underdeveloped possibility. Where this has been done the intention has often been merely to display what a bizarre variety of sounds can be obtained from the human speech organs by the application of contact microphones. An example of such endeavours is the realization by Gordon Mumma and David Tudor of Cage's *Solos for Voice 2* (1960), where the electronic chorus produces an exhibition of noises, few of them recognizably vocal in origin.

A more musically sophisticated exploration of choral microphone singing is provided by Stockhausen's *Mikrophonie II* (1965), where sopranos and basses are ring modulated with a Hammond organ. Whatever the organ plays thus affects the vocal timbres, the technique being similar to that which Stockhausen had recently applied in his *Mixtur* for ring-modulated orchestra. In *Mikrophonie II*, however, the effect is less devastating. The voices remain recognizable, and their words, often speaking of blackness and enclosure are audible for much of the time. But even without them this would be a dark experience, for the hollow range of the small choir (without the middle voices of altos and tenors), coupled with the coarsening effect of the modulation, gives rise to music which is consistently sombre in tone, despite all its textural inventiveness. Unmodulated excerpts from *Gesang der Jünglinge* and other earlier works, appearing from time to time on tape, tend to emphasize by contrast the overbearing cloudiness of the new work.

II.3 Out of the unknown

Much of the most interesting tape music has come not from the use of natural sounds, as in *musique concrète* and works for recorded voices, but rather from the synthesis of new material by electronic means. Until synthesizers became available in the mid-sixties this was a laborious process, requiring a great deal of time and effort in the creation and assembly of sounds, and so it is not surprising that the number of worthwhile 'pure' electronic works composed before 1965 is rather small. Their importance, however, in terms both of their technical innovations and of their radically new contribution to musical experience, is immense. In particular, the works produced by Stockhausen and others at the Cologne studio in the fifties include many of the finest examples of tape music, and one may be led to conclude that the very difficulty of the techniques caused these composers to spend long hours of reflection while working, and so to build in a subtlety of sound and form very often lacking in music composed later on synthesizers.

Work at Cologne was directed by quite specific technical and musical interests. On the technical side, the influence of Werner Meyer-Eppler encouraged composers to look to contemporary research in the phonetics of language, which suggested models for the composition of timbres and which, more directly, resulted in the use of vocal material in such works as Stockhausen's *Gesang der Jünglinge*, Krenek's *Pfingstoratorium* (1956) and Eimert's *Epitaph für Aikichi Kuboyama* (1960–62). The prevailing musical discipline, meanwhile, was that of serialism, especially the extension of serial methods to govern every aspect of sound. Several composers, including Babbitt and Boulez, had already applied serial controls to rhythm in the late forties, but it was difficult to see how the technique could be logically extended to the domain of timbre unless there were to be some way of determining exactly what constituent frequencies each timbre was to contain. The question of timbre synthesis thus became extremely important, and in Stockhausen's *Studie I* (1953) the creation of timbres from individual sine tones, as described in chapter I.2, was essayed for the first time. The sine tones, however, obstinately failed to gel, and so in his *Studie II* (1954) Stockhausen tried a different technique, splicing together groups of sine tones, playing them back together, and recording the reverberation of the mixture; but again the work's success in generating unified timbres is modest.

This does not mean that these early studies are without value, for, as so often, the composer snatches musical worth from the jaws of technical defeat. Unlike most contemporary efforts in *musique concrète*, the studies ask to be heard simply as musical artefacts and not to be enjoyed for their evocative resonances. *Studie I* offers the listener a pure structure in sound, the sine tones creating a surface of ringing chimes and deeper thuds, and the work's structural intricacy, together with its length of nearly ten minutes, calling for a contemplative approach. *Studie II*, by contrast, is brief and dynamic, its scintillating bundles of frequencies leaping about the novel pitch framework which Stockhausen employs (an octave-less system with steps slightly divergent from the semitone).

Dissatisfaction with the colourless sound of sine tones caused some composers to look to other means of electronic sound generation. Pousseur, for instance, created his *Scambi* (Milan studio, 1957) from 'white noise', a uniform mixture of all frequencies which may be heard, for example, when an FM radio is tuned between stations. Instead of creating sounds by additive synthesis, as Stockhausen had done in his studies, Pousseur used a subtractive method, carving out his material by employing filters to remove selectively certain bands of frequencies. In this way he was able to compose a work which plays with opposing sound masses in a stark and decisive manner. The subsequent development in Pousseur's electronic music, from the rough-hewn sculpting of *Scambi* to the sophistication of *Trois visages de Liège* four years later, must be attributed to the enrichment of studio technique achieved in the interim by Stockhausen during the composition of his *Kontakte* (1958–60).

Kontakte is perhaps the electronic work *par excellence*, since in technical and musical respects it is entirely a work of the new medium. As far as technique is concerned, Stockhausen here displays his virtuosity in creating sound of unprecedented richness and interest, assisted by a recent discovery at the Cologne studio. Heinz Schütz, a technician, had altered the sequence of the heads on a tape recorder from the normal erase–record–playback to playback–erase–record; this made it possible for separate sounds to be superimposed automatically on a tape loop, so that a complex sound could be created swiftly, without the need for lengthy processes of cutting and mixing. The technique was used by Gottfried Michael Koenig in his *Klangfiguren I* (1955), but in *Kontakte* it is used over a much vaster span, to create a work of changing soundscapes which plays continuously for over half an hour. And *Kontakte* succeeds in holding the attention for that length of time because the sounds, though purely electronic in origin, have the busy inner life the new technique made attainable.

The work's musical aptness to the medium is a matter of form and conception as much as of material. Stockhausen no longer uses sounds, as he had in the studies, as bearers of abstract quantities (frequency, duration, etc); instead they function as themselves. There are many events which somewhat resemble percussion sounds, and the tape may be played with music for piano and percussion soloists to make such connections clear. But more often *Kontakte* takes its hearers into realms of the unknown and the unnameable, unfolding in sound without reference to physical objects or musical systems. It is a work which invites exploration from the inside rather than observation from without, a kind of listening that is alert to nuances within evolving masses of sound; and it imposes such an approach most effectively when heard, as the composer intended, in four-channel playback (*Kontakte* was indeed one of the first compositions for four-track tape recorder). Only when the listener is surrounded by the sounds can the piece work its grand effects of rotation and answering, but even in a stereo version it projects its sounds as things in motion, partly because of the Döppler effects suggested by pitch changes in static bands of material (as if they were being generated by great engines moving towards and away from the hearer), partly because the sounds grow and change and interact so audibly.

Stockhausen has outlined in a lecture four 'criteria of electronic music', or musical possibilities unique to the medium, and these provide some help in approaching his *Kontakte*. To begin with, electronic music can demonstrate the unity of the basic elements of pitch, timbre and duration. A pitched note will, when slowed down, become a succession of separate beats (this happens when the frequency falls below about sixteen cycles per second), and a collection of pitched notes can be speeded up to produce a single sound whose timbre depends on the original material. All music, one may say, is vibration, from the rapid oscillations which are the highest harmonics of the triangle right down to the slow swells of musical forms. This was, from both aesthetic and creative points of view, an important insight which could not have been made except in electronic music, and *Kontakte* celebrates it. At two points, for instance, pitched sounds dramatically wind down to reveal their origins in distinct pulses, but Stockhausen's 'unity of musical time' can be felt as a guiding principle throughout the piece.

His second characteristic of electronic music is that it alone can demonstrate the composition and decomposition of timbres, and again this takes place on numerous occasions in *Kontakte* where sounds merge into more complex entities or else divide into simpler ones. Thirdly, the work shows a 'differentiation among degrees of intensity' in that, by the regulation of loudness and reverberation, Stockhausen establishes distinct planes of sound, from the very close to the far distant, sometimes with different musical processes taking place simultaneously on separate planes. The fourth characteristic is that of 'ordered relationships between sound and noise', and once more *Kontakte* serves as an example, containing as it does a range of material from identifiable pitches to dense noise, set in a context of mediation rather than contrast.

For those who would, like Stockhausen, regard electronic music as fundamentally different from instrumental music in its potentialities and so demanding quite new modes of thought, *Kontakte* sets a standard of imagination and technical mastery which has rarely been equalled. But many composers have not seen the medium as requiring a radical change of method, even if they have used purely electronic means of sound generation. The tape pieces of Henk Badings, for instance, are not so different from his instrumental works in their contrapuntal, neo-classical style, and the use of electronic means to create quasi-instrumental voices is also to be found in much American electronic music. Mel Powell's *Second Electronic Setting* (1962), for instance, is a brilliant essay in active electronic counterpoint, and Kenneth Gaburo's *Lemon Drops* (1965) comes close to a jazz piano improvisation in both style and timbre.

Electronic music of this instrumental kind became much easier to produce when synthesizers appeared on the market. The synthesizer offers the composer a variety of electronic devices for generating and processing sounds; essentially, much of the apparatus of the classic studio is assembled into one machine, with the added advantage that the equipment can be controlled electronically rather than by hand. (The various devices on a standard Moog synthesizer are well demonstrated on the two records of *The Nonesuch Guide to Electronic Music*, HC 73018.) However, far from enabling composers to develop the techniques of such studio-created works as *Kontakte*, synthesizers have tended to impose quasi-instrumental styles and the use of the conventional twelve-note tempered scale. Walter Carlos's arrangements, published in such popular albums as *Switched On Bach* (1968) and *The Well-Tempered Synthesizer* (1969), have perhaps contributed to the common view of the synthesizer as a kind of super-electric organ.

However, a good many fine works have been composed by the use of instrumental techniques on synthesizers, not only on the voltage-controlled types developed by Moog and others but also on the RCA Synthesizer at the Columbia–Princeton Center in New York. Babbitt, who has used this apparatus in all his electronic works, finds it well suited to his requirements of the medium. He values electronic means not for their ability to generate new sounds but rather for the precise control they admit, particularly in the domain of rhythm. For a composer who has had to make do with ill-prepared performances of his orchestral music, the RCA Synthesizer, which can be instructed to produce exact pitches throughout a range of definable timbres, is obviously a welcome instrument, while the use of tape makes it a relatively easy matter to stipulate durations with accuracy.

Babbitt's two works for tape alone, *Composition for Synthesizer* (1960–61) and *Ensembles for Synthesizer* (1962–4), are among his most cogent works, though they necessarily lack the dramatic flair of his *Philomel* for voice and tape. Both are polyphonic constructions which could, quite imaginably, have been scored for some combination of conventional instruments. There is a keyboard feel to the music, due to the kind of figuration employed but also to the clear separation of treble and bass in the contrapuntal working. As in all Babbitt's music, the surface is densely patterned with reflections and transformations of motif, each work seeming to grow almost spontaneously from a small initial idea working itself out within a tightly formulated system. *Composition* is the easier piece to follow, for here the pace of thought is slower, there are more obvious repetitions and symmetries, and the form, culminating in a climax which shakes at a single chord, is simpler. *Ensembles* is a composite of many tiny and ingeniously worked fragments, beginning with an alternation between short counterpoints and chords from which notes are successively removed (offering some brief comparison with Stockhausen's 'decomposition of timbres'), then continuing as a closely integrated mosaic.

Few other composers have worked successfully with the RCA Synthesizer; indeed, only Charles Wuorinen's *Time's Encomium* (1968–9) can stand with Babbitt's works as a model of what that machine can offer to a composer concerned with precise definition and the elaboration of complex musical forms. Wuorinen's work, lasting for over half an hour, is more outgoing in its appeal than Babbitt's considerably shorter compositions: the difference is that between a symphony and a string quartet. Like Babbitt, Wuorinen prizes the electronic medium for the ability to realize exact rhythmic quantities, and his work is indeed an encomium of time in its attention to rhythmic proportions on the smallest and the largest scale. However, Wuorinen also directs his mind to what he has described as a besetting problem in tape music: the absence of performers to assist the composer in the projection of musical relations, so that 'the forward unfolding of even the simplest forms is seriously impeded'. Certainly this is a real difficulty, so many tape pieces sounding more like aural scores than performances.

In *Time's Encomium* Wuorinen tackles this problem, to a large degree successfully, by creating ideas which contain the momentum of performance, drawing the listener into a work which develops with power and agility, and which has sufficient complexity to engage attention again and again. The composition uses not only pure synthesized material but also synthesized sounds which have been electronically processed, usually with the addition of reverberation. It thus presents the listener with a foreground of clearly defined musical ideas and an outer space of more or less modified sounds. In general the unaltered sounds pursue a steady, straightforward development (the dominant characteristic of side one of the record release), while the processed sounds lead off into decorative digressions (dominant on side two). Wuorinen thus takes advantage of the bilateral symmetry of the disc as a medium – either side may be played independently – in a work which is perfectly calculated for hearing from loudspeakers.

Some of the best music composed on voltage-controlled synthesizers has also been created specially for gramophone records. The Moog synthesizer, which is customarily used with a keyboard attachment, is well adapted to playing quasi-instrumental lines in equal temperament, as in Carlos's arrangements and original works. The Buchla synthesizer, by contrast, produces sounds in response to finger pressure on touch-sensitive plates, and so lends itself to a more flexible kind of working and to the generation of less well-defined sounds. Its particular strengths are exuberantly displayed in the works of Morton Subotnick, whose *Silver Apples of the Moon* (1967) was the first electronic composition commissioned by a record company and not intended in the first place for concert or broadcast performance.

Subotnick's music is rich in sound-imagery and often quite pictorial in its effects. In the case of *Silver Apples of the Moon* the title's quotation from Yeats aptly suggests the glistening bell-like sounds of the close, achieved through broad arcs of development which gain their impetus from the use of the sequencer. This is an electronic device which can repeat a cycle of control voltages over and over again, and so can be used, at its simplest, to provide a continuously repeating figure. However, it is possible for the cycle to be altered, either by the composer's intervention or automatically, so that the sequencer can assist in the synthesis of continuously changing patterns. Such an application of the synthesizer is demonstrated in Subotnick's second composition for records, *The Wild Bull* (1968), whose most dynamic passages, often suggesting hectic jazz improvisation, are produced in this way. *The Wild Bull* is again a work of direct imagery, here centred on braying horn- or trumpet-like sonorities, and it must count among the most effective examples of electronic music as a medium for intuitive tone painting.

Composers who are more concerned with music as an art of abstract speculation have tended to involve themselves not with voltage-controlled synthesizers but rather with computer sound synthesis, since this offers the composer a much wider field of possibilities and a much larger measure of control. It is in this sphere that, since the mid-sixties, much of the most interesting work in pure electronic sound has been done (Stockhausen having composed nothing with electronic sound alone since *Kontakte*), though computers have also had an important place, as in works by Birtwistle and Dodge which have been mentioned, in the analysis and re-synthesis of natural sounds.

Significant work in computer systems for sound synthesis has been carried out in London by Peter Zinovieff (in whose studio Birtwistle has worked) and in Utrecht by Koenig, but the main impulse has come from the United States, and in particular from a group of composers and technicians working at the universities of Princeton and Columbia and at Bell Telephone Laboratories. They have often been concerned, rather in the manner of Babbitt, with highly developed serial composition: such computer-synthesized works as James K. Randall's brief *Quartets in Pairs* (1964), Charles Dodge's *Changes* and Benjamin Boretz's *Group Variations* (1969–73) are typical. All three of these works are conceived for quasi-instrumental lines; indeed, Boretz's piece exists also in a version for chamber orchestra, and Randall's uses computer synthesis only because no natural quartet could provide the wide ranges of pitch he demands in each part. The computer program for a work of this kind would include specifications of the 'instruments' (i.e. of chosen timbres) and of the 'score' (i.e. details of pitches, durations and degrees of loudness); the output from the computer could then be passed through a digital-to-analog converter, transforming the computer's digital language into something which could be recorded in the form of a magnetic tape. As far as the listener is concerned, the works mentioned above are to be heard, to quote Boretz, as 'polyphonic ensemble music': like Babbitt's *Ensembles for Synthesizer*, they challenge the hearer to an exercise of concentrated perspicacity in detecting the subtlest relations of structure.

Even so, Dodge's *Changes* also provides a surface which fascinates on quite an elementary level. Of the music's three basic constituents – flowing counterpoints of lines, irregularly placed chords and percussive interplays – the lines are most conspicuously affected by 'changes'. Every time a chord appears the timbres of the lines are altered: it is as if with each new chord a different colour filter were placed in front of the counterpoint. This ingenious idea, which can be worked out quite easily on the computer, gives an example of the musical profit to be expected from computer sound synthesis. The same composer's *Earth's Magnetic Field* (1970), which derives pitch successions by musically translating indices of change in the magnetic field of the earth, is a more relaxed piece, appealingly diatonic in the first half, polyphonic and twelve-note in the second.

A less intricate use of computer synthesis than any of these is shown in Ussachevsky's *Computer Piece no. 1* (1968), which has diffuse, bell-like sounds to frame a diversity of synthesized and re-synthesized sounds. Also by Ussachevsky, *Two Sketches for a Computer Piece* (1971) are interesting as rare examples of computer music played in real time by means of a keyboard and a link from the computer to a synthesizer. But whether or not computers ever become effective performance instruments, the future of pure electronic music on tape would seem to lie with computed sound.

II.4 The instrument and its double

The combination of live instrumental playing with electronics has proved to be a powerful and versatile one, enabling the composer to overcome in part the fixity of tape music, to relate his work more directly to common musical experience and to extend the capabilities of conventional instruments. An extension of this kind is most obviously achieved when electronic equipment is used to transform an instrumentalist's tone as he plays, but the alternative procedure, that of bringing instruments together with tape, can also seem to take the instruments beyond their natural bounds.

Solo instruments

A large part of the electronic repertory consists of music for solo instrument with tape or live electronics, perhaps because this combination allows the composer to dramatize one of the central facts of electronic music: that it depends on a rapport between man and technology. The simplest examples are those of the 'Music Minus One' kind, where the soloist plays against a recording made by conventional instruments. Vinko Globokar's *Discours II*, for instance, allows performance either by five trombonists or by a soloist with the other parts on tape. But such a piece is, of course, no more (and no less) electronic music than is a recording of a piano duet by a single player in dialogue with his taped image.

It is a different matter when the tape is of electronic music proper. In such cases the tape may just provide a background for the soloist, as happens in Birtwistle's *Four Interludes from a Tragedy* for basset clarinet and tape (1970), where, in each of the pieces, the electronically synthesized accompaniment is fairly stable in sound quality, register and rhythmic character: it may be a cavernous bass of more or less regular groaning sounds (nos 1 and 4) or a texture of upwards-sliding bell rings (nos 2 and 3), but in either event attention is focused on the line of the live soloist.

More often composers will try to sustain a similar degree of interest in both tape and live constituents, as if the tape were the equivalent of the piano part in a duo sonata. A work of this kind is Luening's *Gargoyles* for violin and tape (1960), which takes the form of a set of variations, some for violin alone, some for tape alone and some for both together, with one or the other dominating. One has the impression here of two energetic partners who copy each other's gestures: the tape favours rolling gambols while the violin takes more to high lyrical flights, but it is often through imitation that the sections of the piece are fused.

One kind of mimicry not used by Luening is imitation of timbre, which is subtly and wittily employed in Mario Davidovsky's *Synchronisms*, a series of works for various combinations of live performers and tape. The first, for flute (1963), and the third, for cello (1965), both have sectional forms in which the soloist plays sometimes with and sometimes without the tape. This allows for dialogues of the sort to be found in the Luening piece, but with the added refinement of some common ground of timbre: the tape in *Synchronisms no. 1* includes flute-like sounds, while in *no. 3* the cello uses its whole range of effects in imitating the tape. The sixth of the series, for piano (1970), takes this further and dispenses with clear formal demarcations; it is not a dialogue but a solo for the live instrument, which one becomes tempted to believe capable of the more or less piano-like sonorities that come from the loudspeakers. In this way the range of the instrument is apparently extended without any electronic modification of its tone.

The use of a live soloist with tape can also give rise to more dramatic confrontations, depending less on purely musical discourse, as in Davidovsky, and more on the atmospheric possibilities of the tape medium. Jacob Druckman's *Animus* series, though comparable with Davidovsky's *Synchronisms* in providing vehicles for solo virtuosity, at the same time shows the composer exploiting the mystery and the drama of recorded sound. In *Animus III* (1969) the live clarinettist is challenged to feats of boldness and brilliance, occasionally drawing on electronic means of transformation, and the tape weaves a nocturnal spell, erupting into nightmarishness with brief bursts of laughter at the soloist. Druckman's rather psychological writing for instruments, composing lines which seem to trace states of mind, is to be found also in his *Synapse* → *Valentine* (1970), where the opposed forces of tape and double bass are kept entirely separate. Each half of the work can be played on its own, but when the two are brought together the electronic *Synapse* becomes a prelude to the instrumental *Valentine*, opening up areas of sound which the player must explore. Unfortunately, the bassist's range of timbre is considerably more limited than the loudspeaker's, and so the piece suggests that the live performer is vainly attempting to draw from a recalcitrant instrument the sounds which he has heard in his imagination. Again the combination, though not simultaneous, is a dramatic one.

Examples described so far have shown tape used as a background, an equal partner or a dramatic milieu. One further possibility, exemplified by Dodge's *Extensions* for trumpet and tape (1973), is that the two sources should operate on distinct but parallel lines. Here the elegant trumpet part emphasizes intervals which divide the octave into equal segments, such as the tritone (half an octave) or the minor third (a quarter of an octave). The computer-synthesized sounds on tape also make use of equal pitch divisions, but over a much wider field, and the linear trumpet music is pitched against chords of ever-increasing density, combing through wide registers in sweeping glissandos. The 'extensions' of the title, therefore, are not so much of the instrument, for once, as of the work's fundamental idea, reinterpreted in a wider sphere.

But the tape recorder, instead of being used to relay a prepared tape as in all the examples mentioned so far, can participate directly in the instrumentalist's performance, as it does in Stockhausen's *Solo* (1965–6). The soloist, playing on any melody instrument (e.g. violin, flute, trombone), performs from a notated part, and as he does so his music is recorded on a loop of tape by assistants. This revolves continuously, and so, if nothing more were done, would provide a perpetual ostinato. However, more is done: new live material can be superimposed on the old, and the volume of playback can be altered so that, for example, brief snatches of the recording only are presented. *Solo* thus unfolds as an ever-changing polyphony, with reminiscences and half-memories wrapped around the continuing performance of the instrumentalist, a contrapuntal tissue emerging from an instrument capable only of single lines. In performance the effect can be surprising, even theatrical, but it becomes less so when the work is heard in a recording. To compensate for that in the disc version (made by Globokar on trombone) Stockhausen added a 'commentary' taken from his tape work *Hymnen* – a clever idea, but one which detracts from the experience of *Solo* for the reason that *Hymnen* has such power of its own.

Another piece by Stockhausen, *Spiral* (1968), extends the instrument (or voice) by asking the performer to go 'beyond the limits of the playing/singing technique that you have used up to this point and then also beyond the limitations of your instrument/ voice'. This is one of the instructions which the soloist must apply in imitating and transforming what he hears from a shortwave radio: that is the only electronic adjunct essential to the piece, though performances of *Spiral* have tended to be most frequent on electronic instruments, since they permit a wide degree of overlap with the broadcast sound. Harald Bojé's exciting and amusing recording on the electronium shows this well, but equally striking here is the creative virtuosity the work encourages: Bojé finds his analytic imagination particularly stimulated by such an unpromising chance find as 'I could have danced all night'.

A final possibility, where the combination of a solo instrument with electronics is concerned, is the direct alteration of the instrumental sound by electronic means. This technique is used in Heinz Holliger's oboe concerto *Siebengesang* (1966–7), where, after several sections of mounting expressionist tension, the soloist takes up an instrument with a microphone inserted into it, and his sound suddenly gains in volume and versatility. Ingenious writing for the electronic oboe enables its music to be matched with that for stratospheric violins or abrupt brass with equal ease.

Holliger's work, along with Druckman's *Animus III*, provides an unusual example of electronic modification being used to enlarge the scope of solo instrumental playing within the context of relatively traditional musical thought: in both works electronic extension is the exception, and both are fully written out in conventional notation. Other pieces which use electronic adaptations of a solo instrument, such as Mumma's *Hornpipe* or Stockhausen's *Mikrophonie I*, have their logical place in chapter II.7, on live electronic ensembles.

Ensembles

The concerto-like character which is often present in works for instrument and tape, as in those by Davidovsky and Druckman discussed above, gives way naturally to chamber-musical reciprocity in pieces for ensemble and tape. A clear example of this is given by Berio's *Différences* for flute, clarinet, harp, viola, cello and tape (1958–9), where the electronic part is created by manipulating the sounds of the same quintet of instruments. The work begins with the live ensemble playing alone; only later does the tape enter, rather stealthily, to exhibit 'differences' of altered sonority and reverberation while seeming to extend, rather than contrast with, the human performers.

Stockhausen's alternative version of *Kontakte*, with pianist and percussionist joining the tape, is also a work more of alliance than contest. As Stockhausen remarks, the 'known sounds' of the instruments 'provide orientation, perspective to hearing; they function as traffic signs in the unlimited space of the newly discovered electronic sound world'. Thus it is the electronic music that remains at the centre of interest: the players direct one's attention to specific events in it by 'collecting' sounds as they emerge from the loudspeakers, or by prefiguring events, imitating them or adding a contrasted counterpoint. The music becomes easier to follow and perhaps more impressive – not because the instrumentalists add some 'human' dimension missing in the version for tape alone (there is no need for that), but rather because they widen the scale on which the music operates: the electronic sounds come to dwarf the piano and the percussion battery, including even the mighty tam-tam. This can still be felt in a recording, though the unaided ear may have some difficulty in spotting just which sounds are electronic and which instrumental, for as Stockhausen observes, 'the electronic sounds sometimes approach the known sound to the point where they are confusingly alike'.

Confusion between live and electronic sources, already mentioned with reference to the solo works of Davidovsky, is plainly to be achieved most easily when percussion instruments are taking part, since the timbral resources of the percussion come closest to emulating, in nature as in range, those of tape music. Davidovsky's *Synchronisms no. 5* for percussion quintet and tape (1970) melds the two media so completely that only rarely does the tape betray itself by producing what could not be a live sound. More often it is hard to distinguish, especially in a recording, of course, the electronic contributions from the wide spectrum of sounds excited by various means from a large array of percussion instruments.

But the fusion does not have to extend so far. Arne Nordheim's *Respons I* for two percussionists and tape (1966–7) is concerned more with brilliant live duets against an electronic background which offers relatively static support. And Lejaren Hiller's *Machine Music* (1964), though scored like *Kontakte* for piano, percussion and tape, keeps its forces quite distinct, to be used as a trio in different combinations as the music works through its several sections. Both live and electronic sounds are employed to the characteristic end of generating hammered regular rhythms and ostinatos, which occasionally recall the more primitive aspects of Bartók and which constitute 'machine music' indeed.

As for the application of live electronic transformation to conventional ensembles, that has remained rather unusual. George Crumb has used techniques of this kind in several works, such as his *Black Angels* for 'electric string quartet' (1970), but only in order to bring out special effects which would not otherwise be audible. A more thorough-going work of electronic chamber music is Boulez's '. . . *explosante-fixe* . . .' (1971–, work in progress), which uses complex equipment to modify and to project in space the sounds of eight instruments. The idea is that the apparatus should produce 'an interaction of the parts among themselves' and 'transform the individual quality of a "natural" sound into a neutral collectivity of "artificial" sounds', the electronics establishing some degree of community among instruments of very different timbres.

In that respect Boulez's piece follows up some of the possibilities of timbral alteration suggested by Stockhausen's *Mixtur* for orchestra and electronics. Stockhausen himself, in his later *Mantra* for two pianos and electronics (1970), puts the accent not so much on new timbres as on a new harmonic method. This ambitious work, lasting for about an hour, is based entirely on a melody, or 'mantra', which is the germinal cell of everything in the music, governing even the electronic adjuncts. Ring modulators, as so often in Stockhausen's electronic music, have an important role, modulating piano tones with sine waves to produce often clangorous effects.

It is worth giving some attention to the harmonic principles introduced in *Mantra*. A ring modulator is a device which creates from two inputs an output containing only sum and difference frequencies. Thus if the A above middle C on the piano (440 cycles per second) is ring modulated with a sine wave of an octave below (220 cycles per second), the output will contain frequencies of 660 cycles per second and 220 cycles per second, and so one will hear the lower A along with something closely approximating to the E a fifth above the higher A. In other words, the result will be a consonant interval of an octave plus a fifth. But if the piano now moves up a semitone to Bb (466 cycles per second) while the sine wave remains the same, the output will now contain frequencies of 246 cycles per second (B♮) and 686 cycles per second (about a sixth of a tone below F), and the new result will be a strident dissonance.

This illustration is much simplified, since piano tones contain frequencies other than the fundamental, but it does serve to show the principle. The most important point is that the product is simple when the piano frequency is related to the sine-wave frequency by a simple ratio (2:1 in the first example given) and complex when the frequency ratio is complex (233:110 in the second example). Thus the sine wave can serve as a sort of tonic: the degree of harmonic relation between it and the piano pitch will at every point be measured by the degree to which the modulated output is pure and consonant.

That principle enables Stockhausen to construct in *Mantra* an almost symphonic edifice. As he himself explains: 'In each of the thirteen large cycles of the work, each pianist introduces a sine tone, corresponding each time to the central note around which all the mantra-transformations are centred. . . . Each first and thirteenth note of each recurrence of the mantra are . . . identical to the mirroring sine tone; hence they sound completely consonant, and thus completely "natural" – like piano notes; and depending on the intervallic remoteness of the remaining mantra notes from the mirror note of the ring modulation, the modulated sound sounds more or less unlike the piano. . . . Hence one perceives a continual "respiration" from consonant to dissonant to consonant modulator-sounds.' *Mantra* is one of those rare works which uncover a whole new way of working with sound, and which exhilaratingly explore the territory gained.

Orchestras

Any discussion of music for orchestra and tape must begin with Varèse's *Déserts* (1949–54), the first work of this kind and the most impressive. Varèse limits his objectives by juxtaposing rather than combining the media: there are three electronic 'interpolations' in the course of what is essentially an orchestral composition (it can be played as such without the tape sections). The effect is of windows opening three times onto the alien prospects of electronic music. Aside from a few rhythmic imitations there is little to connect the electronic with the instrumental material; instead the 'organized sound', as Varèse calls it, takes advantage of its freedom to range through spheres closed to the orchestra. The first interpolation seems to refer to the sound world of heavy industry; the second is more concerned with percussive rhythms; and the third, most various of all, includes wide glissandos, piercing high notes and, as in the later *Poème électronique*, the macabre intervention of an organ. All three tape sections make vigorous play with the possibilities of two-channel sound, still a novelty when the work was composed.

Despite all these electronic riches, however, one cannot fail to be struck by how much subtler and more fully developed is the orchestral music. Varèse demonstrates extraordinary skill in handling the technique, paradoxically an electronic one in essence, of timbre composition, here using an ensemble of woodwind, brass and percussion, both tuned and untuned. There are also passages which take up Schoenberg's idea of 'timbre melody', where the same note is passed from one instrument to another. And the structure of the piece depends very much on these single pitches to provide points of rest and to define areas of harmonic combat. The electronic music, by contrast, is often coarse: the windows give onto barren landscapes, perhaps the 'deserts' of the title, which for Varèse signified 'not only physical deserts, of sand, of sea, of mountains and of snow, of outer space, of deserted city streets . . . but also that distant inner space which no telescope can fathom, where man is alone in a world of mystery and essential solitude'.

If, unlike Varèse in *Déserts*, the composer has orchestra and tape sounding simultaneously, this at once raises problems in performance, since the tape unrolls at a constant rate and so dictates the orchestral tempo. But in spite of that many works for orchestra and tape have been written since the mid-fifties. One of the simplest is the *Concerted Piece* (1960) jointly composed by Luening and Ussachevsky, who place the tape very much in the role of concerto soloist. The work is rather charmingly direct, beginning with a grand, heraldic orchestral introduction before the tape's nonchalant entrance, and even including a cadenza for whirling electronic sounds.

Other composers for orchestra and tape have tended to look as much for integration as for the concerto-like opposition of the Luening–Ussachevsky piece. Pousseur's *Rimes pour différentes sources sonores* (1958–9), for instance, is concerned with 'rhyming' the two media, not by straightforward imitation but by allusive connections of timbre, interval and rhythm. The orchestra here is made up of small separated ensembles, suggesting the influence of Stockhausen's then recent *Gruppen* for three orchestras, and the work gains much of its intellectual vitality from the interplay between the ornamented music for these ensembles and the cruder, more dynamic electronic sounds. As in Boulez's withdrawn *Poésie pour pouvoir* for orchestra and tape (1958), the composer's orchestral virtuosity triumphs over the relatively primitive techniques available to him in the electronic studio.

In other works of this kind the tape has a more anecdotal role. This is the case in Nordheim's short and sumptuous *Epitaffio* (1963), where the tape enters only occasionally, bringing sounds which the orchestra mimics. Its most important contribution is that of choral voices: sopranos floating overhead at one point, and at the end male voices in a sustained 'ah'. Henze's *Tristan* for piano, orchestra and tape (1973) adds an electronic component to its most highly charged developments and also introduces the recorded voice of a child reading part of the Tristan story, the orchestra meanwhile holding chords from a certain opera on the same theme. In his Second Violin Concerto (1971), too, Henze includes an electronic recitation, this time the recording of a man reading the poem by Enzensberger on which the piece is based.

These works by Nordheim and Henze (and also Boulez's *Poésie pour pouvoir*) show the use of tape to bring another known sound world, that of choral or speaking voices, into orchestral music. Stockhausen uses the same technique in his *Trans* (1971), a potent and poetic work in which only the orchestral strings, placed behind a gauze and bathed in magenta light, are visible on the platform. Their music, in dense, unchanging chords, is riven by the irregular jolts of a weaving shuttle on tape, while the sounds of the wind and percussion groups are projected electronically from behind screens. The piece is the transcription of a dream, but its working out bears witness to Stockhausen's very conscious proficiency in handling not only orchestral sonorities but also electronic technology.

This is apparent in most of his works for large formations since the early sixties. *Mixtur* (1964–7), for instance, divides the orchestra into five groups – woodwind, brass, percussion, bowed strings and plucked strings – each with an electronic technician who uses a sine-tone generator and a ring modulator to transform the instrumental sounds. The result is not so much a composition as a voyage of discovery, journeying through a whole variety of textures and always coming up with more new sounds to be obtained from this application of live electronics to the orchestra.

The musical inventions of *Mixtur* still remain to be more cogently utilized, for Stockhausen has preferred less disruptive electronic aids in his later orchestral works. Among these are a version of the tape work *Hymnen* in which the unmodulated orchestra is made to respond to sound events from the loudspeakers, the above-mentioned *Trans* and also *Inori* for one or two soloists and orchestra (1974–5), all three pieces showing that, for Stockhausen, electronics have become a quite natural and necessary part of the modern orchestral composer's equipment, as much as they are a part of the recording producer's.

II.5 Rock

Though the traditions and purposes of rock music are quite different from those of the 'art' music which is the main concern of this book, electronic developments in rock merit attention for their intrinsic interest as well as for the influence they have had on avant-garde composers. A great deal of the popular music produced since the mid-fifties could be described as electronic, in that it is created through and for electronic means of handling sound. Popular music has developed singing styles which would be impossible without the microphone; it has also very often depended on amplified instruments, of which the electric guitar still holds pride of place. Moreover, the long-playing record has become the main product of rock music, superseding the live performance and so encouraging musicians to use techniques which are available only in the recording studio.

An early example, provided by a group which could never have performed live, is that of the Chipmunks. They were a vocal 'group' created in 1957 by David Seville, their twittering voices engineered by playing recordings of human singing at double speed. But the Chipmunks must be regarded as an exotic sport within the general stream of evolution in popular music; not for another decade did studio techniques begin to be employed creatively by performers. Then, in 1966, the Beach Boys produced their song 'Good vibrations' by using tape manipulations to achieve a rich density of sound, and in the same year the Beatles used tape loops and recordings played backwards in 'I'm only sleeping' and 'Tomorrow never knows', both from their album *Revolver*.

The Beatles' next LP release, *Sgt Pepper's Lonely Hearts Club Band* (1967), stands as the classic example of the rapid changes taking place in rock music at the time. The tape effects of 'Tomorrow never knows' are here pursued, notably in 'A day in the life', but there is increased complexity too on other planes, of melodic construction, orchestration and poetic language. Unlike most earlier rock records, which had been miscellaneous samplings of new repertory, *Sgt Pepper* is a 'work' which asks to be heard as a coherent song cycle. It is music designed for listening, not dancing, and its subject matter has been opened far beyond the old themes of romantic love. Particularly significant in the present connection is the fact that the Beatles' most electronically adventurous songs, such as 'Tomorrow never knows' and 'A day in the life', are those which speak of experiences with hallucinogenic drugs. 'Switch off your mind, relax and float downstream', sings John Lennon in 'Tomorrow never knows', and the entry into the narcotic wonderland is signalled by bird-like electronic effects on tape.

This use of electronic techniques to express drug experiences is also shown in some of the work of the Velvet Underground, a group established by Andy Warhol in the mid-sixties to perform in a New York nightclub to the accompaniment of 'psychedelic' lighting. But since they were a performance group (the Beatles by the time of *Sgt Pepper* were working exclusively in the studio) they naturally developed live electronic techniques. Their song 'Heroin' (1967), for example, has a progressively racing tempo and increasing electronic feedback to create a metaphor of the drug's action: feedback, normally an unwanted effect caused when the sound of an amplified instrument is picked up by its microphone, comes to glaze the music with a sustained howl. Another Velvet Underground song, 'Sister Ray' (1967), is remarkable not only for its length of seventeen minutes but also for the use of the 'fuzz box', an electronic modulating device, to produce a monolithic distorted sound, thick and heavy in texture, the typical sonority of what came to be known as 'hard rock'.

However, the Velvet Underground could also use electronic instruments to achieve more subtle and differentiated effects, as the electric viola playing of John Cale often demonstrates. Cale was one of the first rock musicians to have had direct experience of avant-garde performance, since he was associated not only with the Velvet Underground but also with LaMonte Young and Terry Riley. An influence from these composers can perhaps be detected in the Velvet Underground's exploration of insistent repetition, notably in 'Black angel's death song' (1969), where Cale's electric viola plays with a single motif in regular patterns.

Other American groups to play an important part in the development of electronic rock included the Grateful Dead, with *Anthem of the Sun* (1967–8), and Frank Zappa and the Mothers of Invention, with *Uncle Meat* (also 1967–8). The Grateful Dead's record has interludes, between the songs, of *musique concrète*, based on the modified sounds of keyboard and percussion instruments. In *Aoxomoxoa* (1969) they refined this technique, making closer links between natural and artificial recordings, and making also a greater use of electronic transformation. 'What's become of the baby' from *Aoxomoxoa* has the voice electronically modulated and also employs tape delay (recording a sound and then playing it back after a defined interval) to build 'vocal ensembles' from the sound of a solo singer.

The Grateful Dead's feedback technique, used with a finesse not to be found in the songs of the Velvet Underground or the wild improvisations of the guitarist Jimi Hendrix, is well displayed in their live-recorded album *Live/Dead* (1968), particularly on the track with the title 'Feedback', where an extraordinary range of sounds is drawn from electric guitars. Jerry Garcia, lead guitarist of the group, has explained how feedback can be used in such playing to aid sensitive microtonal performance, to create sustained tones, to accentuate harmonics and subharmonics, and to give the effect of a note played in reverse (by bringing up the volume gradually from zero, a backwards decay, and then suddenly damping the string to cut the feedback loop).

Zappa is another resourceful musician who has explored the specific potentials of electronic rock, often in music which, like that of the Grateful Dead, extends the dimensions of the rock number well beyond those of the three- or four-minute song. His *Uncle Meat* and other records of the late sixties, in which he performed with the Mothers of Invention, demonstrate a thorough use of studio techniques, including speed change, tape reversal and the use of filters to change timbres. He has also often acknowledged the importance to his work of Varèse, Webern, Stravinsky and other 'classical' masters of the twentieth century.

Such an interest in contemporary 'art' music was not unusual among progressive rock musicians of the late sixties: among the heroes enshrined on the cover of *Sgt Pepper* the face of Karlheinz Stockhausen stares out, and the Velvet Underground's links with Young and Riley have already been mentioned. Cross-fertilization, as distinct from the 'synthesis' misguidedly attempted in joint performances by rock groups and symphony orchestras, was an inevitable outcome. The avant-garde English composers Tim Souster and David Bedford, for instance, have been strongly influenced by rock music and have had their works recorded on rock labels. In some cases – such as that of Bedford or the German rock musician Edgar Froese – only the composer's background can be used to determine whether his music should be classed as rock or art.

From the point of view of electronic technique, however, the rapid development in rock music during the years 1966–9 has not been maintained, and to some extent that must be blamed on the arrival of the synthesizer. It was probably the release of Carlos's popular *Switched On Bach* in 1968 that alerted rock musicians to the potentials of synthesizers; certainly from that year they began to assume an increasingly important role in the most musically elaborate rock, in some cases ousting the electric guitar as the centre of a group's sound world.

Several of the most talented rock musicians to have consolidated their reputations during the seventies, including Keith Emerson (of Emerson, Lake and Palmer), Brian Eno (of Roxy Music and other ensembles) and Rick Wakeman (of Yes), have been keyboard performers who have used synthesizers as more versatile relatives of the electric organ and the electric piano. This has stimulated the evolution of a kind of music, highly polished in sound, where the intangible transformations of the Grateful Dead or the coarse blocks of the Velvet Underground can have no place; instead the emphasis is on feats of instrumental virtuosity and on a knowing use of techniques of record production, such as multi-tracking (mixing together several separately recorded performances). It is not surprising that a reaction to the technological sophistication of much rock music should have come, in 1976, in the form of punk, but it is perhaps surprising that the synthesizer should have restricted rather than widened the field of electronic rock.

However, some musicians have continued to use the electronic medium with free inventiveness. Pink Floyd's album *The Dark Side of the Moon* (1972–3), an acknowledged rock classic, stands out for the force of the sounds created from ensembles of synthesizers, guitars and percussion, and also for the effective use of *musique concrète* tracks as interludes between songs. 'Speak to me' and 'On the run', both from this disc, are miniature sound-dramas of vocal fragments, footsteps, clock sounds and so on. They serve not only to provide contrast but also to heighten the dramatic and musical continuity of the album, which follows *Sgt Pepper* in asking to be heard as a whole.

Rather similar in this respect is a contemporary record by Yes, *Close to the Edge* (1972), which also has 'noise' interludes, though of a more limited kind. Unlike Pink Floyd, Yes depend here on the use of the synthesizer as a spectacular solo instrument, which it is also in the music of Emerson, Lake and Palmer. The suave manner of performance and production in the work of this latter group, coupled with their frequent forays into arrangements of 'classical' music, suggests an ambition towards musical respectability not untypical of the period.

Whereas the earlier phase of electronic rock, in the second half of the sixties, had been dominated exclusively by British and American groups, the early seventies saw a wider spread of innovatory activity; in particular, various German groups, such as Tangerine Dream, began to make important contributions, often departing further from conventions of rock. Tangerine Dream's instrumentation is in itself unusual: they are essentially an ensemble of keyboard players using synthesizers and other electronic instruments; guitars and percussion have a relatively limited part. Often they make use of sequencers to maintain simple ostinatos, these repeating fragments creating a foundation for rich, consonant textures. The group also show a preference for continuous playing throughout a side, and some of their lengthier pieces, such as 'Madrigal Meridian' from *Cyclone* (1978), are wholly instrumental.

Edgar Froese, the leading member of Tangerine Dream, has made several solo records which, though they have been released on rock labels, ought properly to be considered as pure electronic music, comparable more with, say, Pierre Henry than with the Bay City Rollers. The title track of his *Aqua* (1973–4) uses, as one might guess, recorded water sounds, but more typical of the piece, and indeed of Froese's solo music in general, are the passages of synthesized sound in defined strata: slowly revolving bass chords, for instance, underpinning structures of ostinatos and other material. 'Panorphelia', from the same album, employs this method most impressively to build a unified sound organism which gains an ominous character as a result of its departures from even temperament.

Many other leading rock artists of the seventies have similarly worked as solo composer–performers besides working with other musicians. The guitarist Mike Oldfield achieved enormous success with his *Tubular Bells* (1975), in which, rather in the manner of Terry Riley, he uses multi-tracking to enable himself to play a variety of instruments simultaneously. Here the record is a single work, and so it is too in the case of Patrick Moraz's *I* (1976), which, despite its pretentiousness ('*I* Stands for initiation, identity, idealism, integration . . .'), is an interesting attempt to bring together various different kinds of music, including electronic rock, 'classical' keyboard music, a Brazilian chant and *musique concrète*.

Brian Eno, whose musical intelligence is evident in his work with David Bowie and with Roxy Music, is another musician who has produced imaginative solo discs. His *Another Green World* (1975), for example, uses carefully chosen materials and techniques to achieve quite precise musical and evocative effects: on the track 'In dark trees' it is the ingenious tracery of lines, recorded on electric guitar and amplified percussion instruments, which creates the dense, shadowed atmosphere. Eno has also been responsible, through his foundation of the Obscure record label, for promoting the work of contemporary British composers from the experimental wing of the avant-garde (Gavin Bryars, John White and others). His own *Discreet Music* (1975), recorded on Obscure, stands much more with their work than with rock, being based on a pair of melodies in continuous repetition but, thanks to tape delay, ever-changing alignment. The hope of a synthesis between rock and the avant-garde seems no better founded than it was in the sixties, but at least Eno has proved that a sensitive musician can work in both spheres.

II.6 Electronic instruments

Electronically amplified instruments have had a small and occa-sional, but still significant, place in the orchestra ever since Stockhausen included a part for electric guitar in his *Gruppen* (1955–7). The electric organ appears frequently in Berio's orchestra, and the electric guitar, again, makes a resolute entrance in Boulez's *Domaines* (1961–9). But these works, and others in which electronic instruments simply add new tone colours to the orchestral spectrum, can hardly be classed as examples of electronic music. This chapter is concerned rather with works in which electronic instruments have a solo role, or in which they constitute a decisive part of the sound resources.

Among the many electronic instruments of the inter-war period, the ondes martenot has been most successful in gathering to itself a repertory, a repertory containing a sufficient number of major works that the instrument will undoubtedly survive. There are parts for solo ondes in Messiaen's *Trois petites liturgies de la Présence Divine* (1943–4) and *Turangalîla-symphonie* (1946–8), in Honegger's *Sémiramis* (1933) and *Jeanne d'Arc au bûcher* (1935), and in Jolivet's concerto for the instrument (1947). Varèse included two ondes in the final version of his *Ecuatorial* (1934), and the instrument has continued to attract the attentions of composers, particularly in France.

Some of the specific qualities of the ondes, particularly in the domain of tone colour, have been mentioned by Messiaen. 'There is', he has said, 'the characteristic timbre of the instrument, called the "timbre onde", but there are also many others. One of these, which has been much employed because it contains the mystery of instruments of metallic resonance thanks to the presence of a small gong in the sound diffuser, is the "metallized" or "metallic timbre", which produces absolutely terrifying, even harrowing effects when the instrument is played with force, or, on the other hand, unearthly halos when it is played softly. There is also a very interesting group of timbres produced by the "palm"; the palm is a diffuser surmounted by a small lyre whose strings vibrate in sympathy with the tones played. This gives rise to complex sonorities of great delicacy.'

In writing for the ondes Messiaen is careful to indicate which of these various timbres he wants, sometimes by analogy with conventional instruments: horn, spinet, 'oriental clarinet' and so on. He often uses the 'metallized timbre' in roaring glissandos or excited trills; equally characteristic is his use of the gentler sonorities to double the violins at the unison or an octave above, adding a perfumed sweetness to much of the string music of the *Turangalîla-symphonie*. When employed in this last way the ondes martenot can easily sound like some celestial hybrid between the violin and the soprano voice, and in the *Trois petites liturgies* its function is sometimes to effect a liaison between the female chorus and the orchestra of strings.

Varèse's scoring for the instrument is very different. In *Ecuatorial* he places two ondes martenot in an ensemble also containing brass, piano, organ and percussion, the whole accompanying a solo bass or bass chorus in an imprecation of the ancient Maya. Sometimes the bass register of the electronic instrument is used to enforce the chant, but Varèse also exploits its penetrating upper treble, at one point taking it to an E beyond the reach of the piano keyboard. The two new instruments thus substitute for, and excel, the high woodwind of his earlier scores.

Extension of the register available to music was one of the benefits of the electronic medium which Varèse outlined in a lecture of 1939; another was 'the possibility of obtaining an infinite number of frequencies or, if one wishes, of subdivisions of the octave'. Except in siren-like glissandos he did not himself make use of this facility in his writing for the ondes martenot, but the instrument is employed as a source of quarter-tones in Messiaen's *Deux monodies* for solo ondes martenot (1938) and in two withdrawn works by Boulez: the first version of his cantata *Le visage nuptial* (1946–7) and a quartet for four ondes martenot (1945–6).

After these works by Boulez, and Messiaen's contemporary *Turangalîla*, interest in electronic instruments waned as composers began to investigate *musique concrète* and other forms of music on tape. Electronic performance machines were not to regain an important place until a new breed, the synthesizer, arrived in the mid-sixties. Though most synthesizers are not, as has been pointed out, expressly designed for concert use, some have been built or adapted for this purpose, beginning with the synket constructed by Paul Ketoff for John Eaton. Vastly more versatile than the ondes martenot, the synket has capacities for varied timbres, microtonal playing and an almost vocal expressiveness, all fully utilized in the numerous works Eaton has composed for it since 1964.

His *Concert Piece* for synket and orchestra (1967) is a concerto which pits the electronic instrument against two orchestral groups, one tuned a quarter-tone above the other. This enables Eaton to match the synket's subtlety in his orchestral writing, and thus, like several composers who have worked with the medium of orchestra plus tape, to assimilate the electronic to the natural sounds. The expressionist vehemence of Eaton's music comes out more strongly in his vocal compositions, which include *Blind Man's Cry* for soprano, synket and Moog synthesizer (1968) and the *Mass* for soprano, male speaker, clarinet, three synkets, synmill (another small electronic instrument), Moog synthesizer and tape delay system (1970). In the earlier work, according to the composer, the synket provides 'the internal, agonized, existential cry that the blindman himself can no longer utter in the face of the brutal, inhuman poundings of fate in the form of the Moog sequencers'. The soprano voice, here as in the *Mass*, is taken to the limits of its compass in a line which mixes sombre intoning with hysterically agitated song. In the *Mass* the electronic instruments often have a static role, producing drifting clouds of sound; the expressive force of the work is contained in the vocal part and in the virtuoso writing for clarinet. With the help of distorted echoes of voice and clarinet from the tape delay system, however, the conventional sounds can at times be brought close to the electronic.

The use of synthesizers in live performance is much more common in rock than in art music, though they and other electronic keyboard instruments have played an important part in the evolution of that stream of American avant-garde music sometimes referred to as 'minimalist': the music of Terry Riley, Steve Reich and Philip Glass, for example. All of these composers have returned to untroubled consonance and rhythmic regularity by way of electronic instruments, rock and exotic musical traditions; often their music is based on close rhythmic patterning over or against a straightforward ostinato, suggesting influences simultaneously from standard rock techniques and from the music of Bali or West Africa.

Riley is essentially a solo improviser, rather in the manner of an Indian sitarist. The recordings of his *Persian Surgery Dervishes* (1971) demonstrate his art in its purest state, since each is the record of an improvisation, with no help from multi-tracking and other studio techniques. Here Riley uses an electric organ together with a tape system which enables him at times to keep a figure recurring as a ground for further flights. Each improvisation, lasting for about three-quarters of an hour, is based on the same mode; the musical interest lies in the creation and development of tiny patterns within the limits of an unchanging modality and a steady beat. *Poppy Nogood and the Phantom Band* (1968) and *A*

Rainbow in Curved Air (1969), both devised specially for recording and produced by Riley alone by means of multi-tracking, employ a variety of electronic keyboard instruments, together with, in the case of *Poppy Nogood*, a soprano saxophone, again with tape systems to feed material back in repeating figures. Like *Persian Surgery Dervishes*, these pieces are mesmeric in their perpetual repetitions and their slow rate of change. The time scale is that of the east, the ethos that of the American west coast at the time of the hippies and the 'drug culture'.

Not all Riley's music is for electronic means: *In C* (1964), the classic of 'minimalism', achieves the characteristic texture of continuously repeating modal patterns by calling on a live ensemble of any constitution, and *Dorian Reeds* (1966), though originally conceived as a solo piece for soprano saxophone and tape loops, can be played by a group of live musicians (the title has then to be changed according to the forces being used, e.g. to *Dorian Brass* or *Dorian Voices*). Even when no electronics are involved, however, it is clear that the music had its starting point in an electronic phenomenon: the ease with which tape loops can generate endless ostinatos. Riley, indeed, began his work in electronic studios in the early sixties, and however primitive and exotic its references may be, his music emerges directly from a peculiarly electronic discovery.

In this respect the music of Steve Reich is comparable. Reich's early experience was also in the electronic studio, and his first pieces, including *Come out* (1966) and *It's gonna rain* (1965), were composed on tape. It was in these works that he developed his technique of 'phasing', by which two identical musical lines are gradually shifted in time with respect to each other, resulting in the creation of new and unexpected rhythms. In both *Come out* and *It's gonna rain* the given material is a short spoken phrase, and phasing not only obliterates the verbal sense but also produces new sounds from the coalescence of phonemes. Reich went on to apply the same basic principle, that of setting off cycles of repeating figures which slowly move out of phase with each other, to the live medium in his *Phase Patterns* for four electric organs (1970). The first player introduces a short motif using two chords and is joined by the second in unison with him. Then the second player begins very gradually to increase his speed, so that the figures move out of phase, and the third and fourth players pick out patterns resulting from the new superimpositions. The piece ends when the second player has gained on the first by a complete bar, and so the two are back in synchrony.

Four Organs, another piece written in 1970 for the same combination (with the addition of a maracas player as time-keeper), also grew directly from work in the tape medium. As Reich has explained: 'The original idea for *Four Organs* came out of an electronic musical device I built in 1968 and '69 with the help of an engineer from Bell Laboratories. This device, the Phase Shifting Gate, could gradually alter the phase position between a number of continuously pulsing tones. If all the tones were in phase (pulsed at the same instant) a repeating chord would be heard. If the tones were moved slightly out of phase a repeating melodic pattern would result.' *Four Organs*, like *Phase Patterns*, is a work built entirely from one simple technical idea. The four organs begin with jabbed repetitions of a chord. Then, very slowly, one note after another is lengthened, with the result that continuously changing melodic figures are drawn out of the chord. Eventually the elongations proceed so far that the music congeals into a sustained sounding of the chord.

To quote the composer again: '*Four Organs* is an example of music that is a "gradual process" . . . . The distinctive thing about musical processes is that they determine all the note-to-note (sound-to-sound) details and the overall form simultaneously.' 'I want', he continues, 'to be able to hear the process happening through the sounding music. To facilitate closely detailed listening, a musical process should happen extremely gradually.' Reich has also noted that: 'It's quite natural to think about musical processes if one has frequently worked with electro-mechanical sound equipment.' Many of his later works, such as *Drumming* (1971) and *Music for Mallet Instruments, Voices and Organ* (1973), make very little or no use of electric instruments, but it was the electric organ which provided the main bridge from studio composition to work with a regular ensemble of musicians. For the electric organ, with its uniform timbres and its capacity to sustain tones indefi-nitely, is peculiarly suited to Reich's kind of process composition.

Philip Glass, who, like Reich, has worked in the main with his own group of performers since the late sixties, has also been concerned with gradual musical processes happening in homogeneous textures of rapid even motion, and has, more consistently than Reich, preferred to work principally with electronic instruments. One fundamental idea in his music, to be found, for instance, in his *Contrary Motion* for electric organ or *Music in Fifths* for ensemble (1969), is the interpolation of tiny repetitions within continuous revolutions of a melodic figure, so that what one hears is a bright, smooth musical surface broken every now and then by miniature cracks. The suite *North Star* (1977) shows this process simplified and glamorized for the purposes of film music. Here Glass uses an ensemble of electronic keyboard instruments (organ, piano, synthesizer), woodwind (saxophones, flute) and voices, in music which frequently proceeds simultaneously on different levels of tempo: an even quaver motion, for example, might be underpinned by a repeating bass in minims, or there might be three distinct planes of activity. As a result, and given also Glass's penchant for the pure consonances of octave and fifth, there is often a hint of medieval organum or else of Balinese gamelan.

It is noteworthy that the composers discussed in these last pages have preferred to work either as solo performers (Riley and Glass) or as directors of their own ensembles. As Glass has put it: 'At present I relate to my music as a composer and performer and have little interest in performance of my music outside of this ensemble. . . . I am conscious of creating a repertory for a specific group of players.' This sort of musical specialization, perhaps inevitable when composers demand quite particular skills of precision or intuitive accord, is a significant phenomenon of the sixties and seventies, affecting not only groups working with electronic instruments but also the live electronic ensembles to be considered in the chapter which follows.

II.7   Live electronic ensembles

The contribution of electronic technology to musical performance has been notable not only in the creation of new instruments but also in the work of live electronic ensembles, by which is meant groups calling on a wide variety of electronic and other equipment in order to make music. Such groups may, according to the tastes of their members, use conventional instruments or voices with or without amplification, electronic instruments (of standard manufacture or else specially built) and all manner of other devices – microphones, amplifiers, modulators, filters and so on – to generate and transform sounds. A live electronic ensemble has, potentially at any rate, the same freedom as the composer in an electronic studio to use any conceivable sound, with the advantage that human subtleties of control are immediately involved. Of course, that may not be regarded as an advantage, in which case the composer will probably prefer the more easily defined sound worlds of synthesizers, computers and electronic instruments.

The work of a live electronic ensemble naturally involves a good deal of experiment in building instruments and circuits for special purposes, in finding sounds required and in developing a feeling of ensemble. Moreover, it is difficult to notate sound events which result from devices and performance techniques that have not been standardized. All this has encouraged ensembles very often to concern themselves with more or less free improvisation, and even where this has not been the case, live electronic ensembles have tended to evolve their own styles and their own repertories. Comparisons can be made more readily with rock groups and jazz bands, where similarly the performers' ideas dominate the composer's, than with classical ensembles such as the string quartet. The evolution of live electronic music has been directed principally by composer–performers working with regular ensembles.

Discussion must begin, nevertheless, with Cage, who, though he has not worked with or written for a particular group, has had a marked influence on the techniques and aesthetics of live electronic music. Indeed, his *Imaginary Landscape no. 1* (1939) might be counted the first work of this kind, even though it was composed for broadcast rather than concert performance. It is a short piece, scored for gramophone records of constant frequencies played on variable-speed turntables (and so giving the effect of sirens), a cymbal and a piano muted by placing the fingers on the strings or played with a gong-beater inside the instrument. Like Cage's works of this period for prepared piano or more normal percussion ensemble, the music is strictly composed on a framework of durational proportions: rhythmic units, rather than melodies and harmonies, are the principal stuff of the piece.

This is also the case in Cage's electronic works of the early forties, where often the electronics are again an extension of the percussion, providing more odd sounds to be assembled in vaguely Balinese grids. The polyrhythmic *Imaginary Landscape no. 3* (1942), for instance, requires six musicians to play on normal percussion instruments and also on an audio frequency oscillator, an electric buzzer, frequency recordings and an electronically amplified marimbula (an instrument of the xylophone family). As in *Imaginary Landscape no. 1*, there is no pitch notation; performers on the oscillator and frequency recordings simply have indications of when and in which direction to make glissandos.

Another work of the same kind, *Credo in Us* (1942), is still more radical, for here the resources include a radio and a gramophone playing something from the classics. Cage suggests Dvořák, Beethoven, Sibelius or Shostakovich; the only commercial recording uses the 'New World' Symphony. Since the player at the gramophone has to raise and lower the needle in accord with the rhythmic quantities Cage has devised, the standard classic is subjected, not without a touch of humour, to piecemeal presentation in a quite alien context, being heard along with exotic, rigid rhythms from two percussionists and a pianist; there is a feeling that the revered masterpiece has been taken into a new world where it must fend for itself with Balinese rhythms and jazz. Nothing could better demonstrate Cage's distance from the great European tradition, a distance which allowed him in later electronic pieces to depart utterly from the notion of the musical work as a unique vehicle of thought.

What Cage presents instead, very often, is a situation in which performers and audience may make their own discoveries quite independent of the composer. This is of the essence in his *Cartridge Music* (1960), a belated return to live electronic music which had the effect of stimulating the whole development of the medium. By this stage Cage had long abandoned the intricate rhythmic structures of twenty years before; the performance materials now consist of a set of transparent plastic sheets, to be laid over each other and so to make, in Cage's words, 'a complex of points, circles, biomorphic shapes, a circle representing block time, and a dotted curving line'. 'Readings are taken', the composer continues, 'which are useful in performance, enabling one to go about his own business of making sounds.' And this is done by inserting such objects as toothpicks and piano wires into gramophone cartridges, or else by manipulating other objects, such as pieces of furniture, which have contact microphones attached to them. The result is a miscellany of bizarre and very often unpleasant noises. 'All sounds', Cage notes, 'even those ordinarily thought to be undesirable, are accepted in this music', and one may take that as a boast or a warning.

The aural experience of *Cartridge Music* is bound to be something of a trial, even though any performance will result in amusing points of theatre, as when a minute action on the part of the performer generates a grotesque outburst of noise, or when one player at volume controls fades another to silence. Beyond that, the piece had importance as a stimulus to other composers. Stockhausen's response came in the very much more sophisticated *Mikrophonie I* (1964), while younger American composers, too, were encouraged to look at the potentials of live electronic music, even if few of them were to emulate Cage in his democratic willingness to open his music to all sounds.

Cage himself has drawn on the experience of *Cartridge Music* in several later works for live electronic forces. The version of his *Variations II* (1961) made by his long-standing associate David Tudor uses the piano as a reservoir of sounds, beautiful resonances and ugly scrapes, to be drawn out by means of gramophone cartridges and contact microphones. *Music for Amplified Toy Pianos* (1960) is self-explanatory, and *Atlas eclipticalis* (1961), which has eighty-six instrumental parts 'to be played in whole or in part, any duration, in any ensemble', can be performed with the instruments amplified. *Atlas eclipticalis* is unusual among Cage's works of the sixties in including some almost conventional notation (pitches obtained by placing star maps across the staves). More often his music from this period is highly indeterminate, and its qualities may be obscure to those who cannot accept Cage's unwillingness to make choices. It is, of course, open to performers to make a 'beautiful' realization, but the most authentic recordings, such as Tudor's of *Variations II*, oblige the listener patiently to accept the boring and the hideous as well.

The published materials for many of Cage's works can give little impression of the musical products to be expected from them, and so, in the absence of frequent live performances, recordings assume an unusually important role in communication. It may be deemed unfortunate, therefore, that few of Cage's pieces have been recorded in more than one performance. Indeterminate scores which have been recorded more than once – such as Earle Brown's graphic design *Four Systems* (1954), performed by the live electronic ensemble Gentle Fire (EMI Electrola C 065 02469) and by the Ensemble Musica Negativa under the composer's direction (EMI Electrola C 165 28955) – prove themselves astonishingly versatile. The 'work' in such cases is the particular performance: it has no separate existence, and one cannot, as perhaps one can in the case of a Beethoven symphony, postulate some ideal performance to stand as a model.

In the case of live electronic music, even where the intention is not so indeterminate, recordings must always have a special documentary value, for reasons suggested earlier, and it is unfortunate that few ensembles are well represented in record catalogues. For example, little of the repertory of Nuova Consonanza and Musica Elettronica Viva, two groups founded in Rome in the mid-sixties, exists on disc, and yet these ensembles did important initiating work in the medium. Both were international and flexible in personnel. Nuova Consonanza tended to favour conventional instruments and voices, sometimes with tape collages as well, but Musica Elettronica Viva were more wide-ranging in their choice of sound sources. As one publicity statement put it: 'Tapes, complex electronics – Moog synthesizer, brainwave amplifiers, photocell mixers for movement of sound in space – are combined with traditional instruments, everyday objects and the environment itself, amplified by means of contact mikes, or not. Sounds may originate both inside and outside the performing–listening space and may move freely within and around it. Jazz, rock, primitive and Oriental musics, Western classical tradition, verbal and organic sound both individual and collective may all be present.'

The aims of Musica Elettronica Viva suggest a view of music as social therapy. *Spacecraft*, an improvised group composition performed during 1967 and 1968, was intended to lead each player from his 'occupied space' of personal inclination to 'a new space which was neither his nor another's, but everybody's'. The recording of this piece, slow-moving and opening strangely at odd moments into silence, does not make it clear that this reorientation has been worked, and the group went on to techniques 'which were more open, more accessible to the casual visitor or listener'. The words, here and above, are those of the group member Frederic Rzewski, who took a lead in loosening the boundaries between performers and audience. His *Free Soup* (1968) and *Sound Pool* (1969) created situations in which everyone was free to participate, the 'musicians' being asked 'to relate to each other and to people and act as naturally and free as possible, without the odious role-playing ceremony of traditional concerts'.

Unlike the two Rome-based groups, the English ensemble AMM, formed at roughly the same time, was inward-looking and concerned exclusively with free improvisation. Three of the members were jazz musicians; the other two, Cornelius Cardew and Christopher Hobbs, came from 'straight' musical backgrounds (Cardew had been an assistant to Stockhausen). But, as demonstrated in a single commercial recording of their music, they were able to sink their differences in improvisation of hypnotic effect. The piece makes much use of sustained sounds, and the ritual atmosphere is heightened by regular gong strokes and other periodic rhythms, while there is some hint of Indian influence in the steady development to a climax in the latter part – though this kind of form seems to result all too readily in improvisations by a regular ensemble.

Another group formed during the mid-sixties, and one recorded much more frequently than any mentioned hitherto, is the ensemble which performs under Stockhausen's direction. Stockhausen first assembled a live electronic ensemble for his *Mikrophonie I*, in which the sole sound source is a large tam-tam, stroked, rubbed and beaten by two performers with various objects while another two use microphones to pick up the resulting vibrations; two further musicians are needed to operate filters and volume controls. By contrast with Cage's *Cartridge Music, Mikrophonie I* is scrupulously notated: the score specifies the kind of sound required, the means of production, the rhythm, the loudness and the electronic controls to be applied. Again, the work is formally determined, for though 'the order of structures may vary considerably from version to version', and 'strong and directional form' is guaranteed by a scheme of permitted connections among the structures.

As a result, and most particularly in a recording, *Mikrophonie I* presents itself as a superior sort of *musique concrète* rather than an anarchic congregation of noises or an exercise in improvisatory virtuosity. Stockhausen demonstrates that 'sound objects', to use Schaeffer's term, can be produced in abundant variety through a straightforward use of live electronic means (there is no modification of the sounds beyond filtering and amplification), while the contrast of duration – *Mikrophonie I* lasts for close on half an hour, whereas Schaeffer's and Henry's early studies had been of three or four minutes – suggests the confidence and scale of the achievement. By limiting himself to a single source Stockhausen ensures that all the sounds of the piece have some acoustic relationship with each other, however tenuous, and his involvement of live performers makes possible a physicality of gesture that had proved very difficult to obtain in the electronic studio.

Mikrophonie I is best approached not as a piece of ensemble music but as a work in the tradition of *Kontakte*, a work in which the sounds themselves are the actors. Like *Kontakte*, the piece consists of a sequence of 'moments', each distinguished by one or more prevailing sound characteristics, the sequence emphasizing at different times relationships of closeness or contrast (or perhaps better, complementarity) between moments. And as so often in Stockhausen's music, his studies in phonetics have left their mark. Not only does the tam-tam sometimes come up with sounds of a surprisingly vocal nature, but also, as Robin Maconie has pointed out, 'a comparison may be made between the voice's continuous modulation of a characteristic resonance [that of the vocal cavity], injecting percussive consonants at points of transition, and *Mikrophonie I*'s process of excitation, amplification and filtering'. The work is thus a 'speech' in which the tam-tam, superficially a rather limited instrument, demonstrates the range of its capabilities.

Stockhausen's experience with *Mikrophonie I* led immediately to his application of electronics to more conventional resources: the orchestra in *Mixtur* and a small chorus in *Mikrophonie II*. Then followed *Prozession* (1967), the first of several pieces written for the ensemble which had been performing *Mikrophonie I* and a work originally scored for tam-tam, viola, electronium (an electronic performance instrument), piano and electronics. What Stockhausen here provides is not a composition but a process, in that there is no notated score. Instead, knowing that he is working with musicians who are familiar with his music, the composer asks them to draw on their knowledge of his earlier works: the tam-tam offers memories of *Mikrophonie I* (it would be difficult to avoid this, since that work is so thorough an exploration of the instrument), the viola alludes to *Gesang der Jünglinge, Kontakte* and *Momente,* the electronium to *Telemusik* and *Solo,* and the piano to *Kontakte* and the cycle of piano pieces. All these references are woven into a fabric of largely intuitive playing, for the instrumental parts contain only general signs indicating how each player must react to what he himself or somebody else has just played. For example, a plus sign stipulates that the new event must be higher or louder or longer or more complexly divided, and the meanings of the other principal signs, minus and equals, are correspondingly wide.

The sequences of signs in the four parts guarantee certain relationships among the players, and the ensemble feeling is further strengthened by directions at some points that one player is to take the lead in some defined manner; everyone may be asked for instance to imitate the intensity of the tam-tam. Quite unlike *Mikrophonie I,* therefore, *Prozession* is a piece of chamber music for a quartet of cooperating individuals. Its scheme is flexible enough to permit each player to use his own imagination, yet strong enough to impose typical Stockhausen features of constant change, mediation between extremes, and disguised symmetry. Also, of course, the origin of the raw materials in his own music ensures some degree of stylistic consistency, while at the same time allowing for surprising combinations, juxtapositions and extensions. The appreciation of these may require a secure familiarity with Stockhausen's earlier output, but the musical developments as such remain open to the innocent ear, if it be also alert. The history of Musica Elettronica Viva suggests their awareness that music of a largely improvisatory nature could, without anything corresponding to the agreed conventions of most jazz or Indian music, easily seem meaningless to its audience. Stockhausen surmounts that difficulty. He provides in *Prozession* a frame of reference, that of his own music, but also, and more importantly, a process which brings with it a variety of musical conversations and soliloquies.

In his next work for his live electronic ensemble, *Kurzwellen* (1968), Stockhausen makes the musical process even more open.

Once more the parts consist mostly of alphabetical signs, but now the source material is not the players' internal memories of Stockhausen's oeuvre; instead they react to the external material, audible to the audience, of sounds received from shortwave radios. 'What I have composed', Stockhausen explains, 'is the process of transforming: *how* they react to what they hear on the radio; *how* they imitate it and then modulate or transpose it in time – longer or shorter, with greater or lesser rhythmic articulation – and in space – higher or lower, louder or softer; *when* and *how* and *how often* they are to play together or alternately in duos, trios or quartets; *how* they call out to each other, issue invitations, so that together they can observe a single event passing amongst them for a stretch of time, letting it shrink and grow, building it up and spreading it out, darkening it and brightening it, condensing it and losing it in embellishments.'

The disposition of signs in *Kurzwellen* encourages a more enclosed feeling of ensemble than was the case in *Prozession*. Where the earlier work had striven to stimulate each player's inventiveness in developing the basic material, *Kurzwellen* proposes a communal meditative approach, the four players collaborating to gather and discuss the transmissions they receive. And since the radios are shortwave receivers, those transmissions are most likely to consist largely of 'electronic' effects ('static', morse signals, speech and music heavily disguised by modulation) rather than intelligible programmes, and so one has the impression that the performers are tuning into a universe of sounds, not trying to pick up stations. This is even true of the special version of *Kurzwellen*, recorded as *Opus 1970*, which Stockhausen made to celebrate the bicentenary of Beethoven's birth. Here the shortwave receivers are replaced by tapes of music and prose by the great predecessor, but so thoroughly transformed by electronic means that they sound like shortwave broadcasts.

Recordings of *Prozession, Kurzwellen* and *Opus 1970* exhibit an extraordinarily successful balance, very rare in live electronic music, between conscientious ensemble playing and exhilarating discovery; the listener is encouraged to attend to a musical dialogue, but he is also repeatedly surprised by the unexpected sound. Stockhausen's programme note for the first performance of *Kurzwellen* concludes with the words: 'We have come to the edge of a world which offers us the limits of the accessible, of the unpredictable; it must be possible for something not of this world to find a way through, something that hitherto could not be found by any radio station on this earth. Let us set out to look for it!' The tone may be a shade dramatic, but undoubtedly *Kurzwellen* is a process which allows for the appearance of the unknown, whether from a radio receiver or from a player's intuitive response – which response is, in performances by Stockhausen's own ensemble, filtered by the composer's operations at the controlling console.

Stockhausen's autocratic rule over his players, which contrasts markedly with the perfect democracy sought by such groups as Musica Elettronica Viva, is perhaps the key to the distinctive, flexible and integrated, completely professional style to be found in most of the many recordings by his ensemble. Another important factor must be their exclusive adherence to Stockhausen's music. In the early years their repertory included pieces by other members, such as Johannes G. Fritsch's *Partita* for viola and electronics (1965–6), but since the departure of Fritsch and Rolf Gehlhaar in 1970 they have played only Stockhausen.

Such dedication may be helpful for the adequate performance of *Prozession*, and even necessary in the case of two later sets of pieces, *Aus den sieben Tagen* (1968) and *Für kommende Zeiten* (1968–70), in which Stockhausen presents only short prose poems as spurs to intuitive music making. 'By *intuitive music*', Stockhausen has written, 'I mean to stress that it comes virtually unhindered from the intuition, and that as music, in the case of a group of musicians playing intuitively, it amounts to more, qualitatively speaking, than the sum total of individual "accidents", by virtue of a process of mutual "feedback". The "orientation" of musicians, which I call "accord", is not, I would emphasize, random or merely negative – in the sense of exclusive – musical thought, but joint concentration on a written text of mine which provokes the intuitive faculty in a clearly-defined manner.'

What Stockhausen expects from an intuitive performance, therefore, is not free improvisation, which he has condemned, but rather a collective musical contemplation. The pieces of his two poetic anthologies are notionally available to any ensemble, but they have generally been regarded as part of the repertory for live electronic ensemble, and Stockhausen has directed few performances with other than his own group, sometimes with additional members. *Prozession* and *Kurzwellen* thus become preparatory exercises, defining group interplay in quite specific terms and leading the group towards the communal approach needed for the text pieces. One may also note, in listening to the recordings of these pieces made under Stockhausen's supervision, how often the players draw on their experience of previous Stockhausen works to provide even the musical material of their performance. Many of these recordings were made without prior rehearsal, so it is claimed, and yet one is bound to wonder just how much influence the composer exerted over what was to happen.

This question presents itself most forcibly when there is the opportunity to compare two recorded performances of the same piece. We have that opportunity with *Verbindung*, from *Aus den sieben Tagen*, which was recorded by an ensemble under Stockhausen's control in Paris in June 1969 (Musique Vivante MV 30795) and then again by the same players in Darmstadt two months later (DGG 2720 073). This piece asks each musician to play 'vibrations in the rhythm of' his body, his heart, his breathing, his thinking, his intuition, his enlightenment, and the universe; the seven rhythms are then to be freely mixed. Inevitably, both performances abound in the regular rhythms of walking, of the heartbeat and of breathing, but what is more striking, because less predictable, is the degree of formal similarity between the two versions. Both last for about 24½ minutes, both oscillate between sustained climaxes and falls to near silence, and there are even close resemblances of detail: in each performance, for example, a sequence of decisive piano chords serves to re-instigate motion at one point, this starting at about 9′ 13″ in the earlier recording and 9′ 50″ in the later. It must be said that the second performance is a great deal subtler and more assured, but the similarities suggest either some planning or a surprising congruence of intuitive response.

The more important considerations, however, are those of quality, and on that count the recordings from *Aus den sieben Tagen* and *Für kommende Zeiten* constitute the most consistently beautiful and interesting body of music for live electronic ensemble available on disc. This is music which demands patience, for the 'rhythm of enlightenment' is sometimes slow; but the players' concentration frequently leads them to ensemble textures of high intensity or gleaming accord, and to imaginative flights which could not have been achieved in a more bounded medium or with a more prescribed manner of composition. There is also great variety of form and gesture, from the wide-spaced openness of *Unbegrenzt*, with long passages of mystical recitation by the composer, to the more objective manner and the complex exotic rhythms of *Ceylon*.

Although Stockhausen's own ensemble have given the most accomplished and stylish performances of his text compositions, the existence of this repertory, and also of *Prozession, Kurzwellen* and other works, has stimulated the formation of other groups, such as the English ensembles Intermodulation (1969–76) and Gentle Fire (1968–76). These, together with his own players, were among the musicians invited by Stockhausen to take part in his *Sternklang* (1971), in which he took advantage of the aptness of live electronic music to spectacular locations: the work is to be played in a public park 'during the warm summer weather, under a clear starry sky, preferably at a time of full moon'. Here the meditation of the earlier works for live electronic ensemble is extended to the scale of a public celebration of harmony, with five groups tuning themselves to specified chords, communicating with each other through musical signals and torch-bearing runners, and at times chanting the names of the constellations.

Sternklang might be taken as a manifestation on a larger scale of the 'rhythm of the universe' (and the harmony) of which Stockhausen had spoken in *Verbindung*; the later *Ylem* (1972) is a simple picture of that rhythm in its grandest dimension. Scored for four electronic instruments and conventional ensemble, this little piece presents in miniature the presumed oscillation of the universe from 'big bang' out to a distant spreading and back to a single point. The players all begin on the platform, reiterating an A or an E♭, then depart to take up positions around the hall and to range over the whole spectrum of pitch; after eleven minutes of gradual deceleration the process is reversed. Meanwhile the electronic instruments, remaining on the platform, project glissandos and so link one player to another.

The recordings of *Sternklang* and *Ylem*, both of which include members of the two English ensembles as well as the composer's own group, bear witness to a common approach engendered by Stockhausen's dominating position in live electronic music, and his influence is to be found in much of the work of younger composers. For example, Tim Souster's *Spectral* for viola and electronics (1972), the only piece from Intermodulation's original repertory to have been recorded commercially, could not have existed without Stockhausen's *Solo* and without Fritsch's demonstrations of the electric viola's capacities in his work with the Stockhausen ensemble. The influences are positive, in that *Spectral* is a fine and colourful lament evocative of whale songs, but they are unmistakable. However, Souster's later work with the ensemble 0dB (zero decibels), founded in 1976 from the remnants of Intermodulation, draws much more from his experience of electronic rock.

Gentle Fire, who took their name from a Buddhist term for the spirit which holds a group together, also showed the mark of Stockhausen in their music, but they were influenced in addition by Musica Elettronica Viva, Cage and other American musicians. Shapely and smoothly integrated, their performances often made use of specially constructed instruments with as much visual as sonorous appeal, and they owed their close corporate identity to a feeling of comradeship rather than to the dominance of any one member: much of their best work came in the form of group compositions or collective interpretations of libertarian pieces by Stockhausen, Cage, Brown or Christian Wolff.

The American group Sonic Arts Union, similarly democratic in their working style, differ from their European colleagues in concentrating on compositions by members, those members being Robert Ashley, David Behrman, Alvin Lucier and Gordon Mumma. Their activities arose from work carried out by Ashley and Mumma at the Cooperative Studio for Electronic Music in Ann Arbor, Michigan, and they began to give performances together in 1966. Much of their repertory consists of solo pieces, each composer performing his own work, and very often the music arises quite naturally and inevitably from a particular assembly of electronic and natural sound resources. An example is Behrman's *Wave Train* (1966), a feedback piece in which magnetic guitar pick-ups are attached to the strings of a piano and loudspeakers placed so that they cause the strings to vibrate. Thus a vibration can be picked up, amplified, projected through a loudspeaker, and so made to prolong itself. Ashley's *The Wolfman* (1964) also uses feedback, here to add a grotesque dimension to vocal sound.

More sophisticated electronic devices have been developed by Mumma, for whom circuit design is an integral part of the creative process. Several of his works, such as *Hornpipe* for horn and electronics (1967), employ his own 'cybersonic consoles' to alter sounds in often curious ways. In the particular case of *Hornpipe*, the sound of the instrument is altered acoustically by the substitution of reeds for the conventional mouthpiece, so that it becomes impossible to distinguish the natural from the electronically treated sound. The same composer's *Cybersonic Cantilevers* (1973) charmingly makes such circuitry available to the audience, who can bring their own sounds, live or recorded, and witness the transmogrifications to which they are subjected.

Lucier's most characteristic work has been intimately concerned with the acoustic space in which it is performed. This is so in the case of *I am sitting in a room* (1970), mentioned in chapter I.2, but his purest work of this kind is *Vespers* (1968). Here the performers walk blindfolded about a darkened room, carrying with them click generators and listening to the echoes so that, bat-like, they avoid colliding with each other or with stationary objects. They must also alter the speed of the clicks so that echoes come exactly halfway between them, and thus each performer takes 'slow sound photographs of his surroundings'.

In general, as in the particular case of this Lucier piece, the work of the Sonic Arts Union may be described as exploratory. The concern is not so much with creating a musical composition as with making an adaptable process. And where Stockhausen's musical processes usually have a residual formal identity for all their openness (as we have seen, this appears to be true even of his text compositions), the Sonic Arts Union develop processes which depend on particular configurations of technology rather than structural principles. It is open to a live electronic ensemble to investigate unlimited ways in which the musician can work with technology, but it is Stockhausen's music that sets the standards by which the artistic success of the collaboration can be judged.

II.8 The music of the world

If the world can now be considered, in McLuhan's celebrated phrase, a 'global village', then it is by way of the electronic media that we learn the gossip of the green. A radio receiver gives anyone access to the musical cultures of distant times and places, and the experience is common of twiddling the tuning knob, preferably after nightfall, to hear a mélange of speech and music, of fragments jostling with each other, mixed without meaning and often distorted by modulation. It would be surprising if this great ragbag of sound, and what it implies about the flexibility of our imaginations, had not touched composers of electronic music. In fact, the electronic flux has become a central image in much creative work, particularly in the United States, where Charles Ives was making musical collages before Marconi.

Several of the electronic works of Cage, in particular, seem like attempts to reproduce the chaos of transmissions that can be heard when one toys with a radio set. His *Williams Mix* (1952), the earliest tape collage, combines eight tracks made up of snippets in six categories: 'city sounds', 'country sounds', 'electronic sounds', 'manually produced sounds, including the literature of music', 'wind-produced sounds, including songs' and 'small sounds requiring amplification'. But Cage was not intending to re-create the electronic hubbub, or indeed intending at all. Like much of his work since the beginning of the fifties, *Williams Mix* is an essay in non-intention, in creating opportunities for listening rather than manufacturing a finished product. The 'real' *Williams Mix* is not the tape, a fixed entity, but rather the score which shows how sounds in the various categories are to be spliced together.

In describing the influence of McLuhan on his music, Cage has remarked that: 'New art and music do not communicate an individual's conceptions in ordered structures, but they implement processes which are, as are our daily lives, opportunities for perception (observation and listening).' Throughout the fifties and sixties Cage was to make such opportunities ever more open. In *Fontana Mix* for tape (1958) he does away with the detailed prescriptions of *Williams Mix* and substitutes graphic designs, as in the later *Variations* series, these allowing abundant freedom of interpretation to those who must make the mix of multifarious recorded materials. And the score of *Rozart Mix* (1965) consists merely of an exchange of letters with Alvin Lucier, proposing that at least eighty-eight tape loops, of unspecified sounds, be played on at least a dozen tape recorders.

Cage has undertaken similar work with radio equipment. His *Imaginary Landscape no. 4* (1951) requires two operators on each of twelve radios, one to regulate the tuning dial and one the volume control. The score scrupulously notates wavelengths and dynamics – an ironic precision when the composer cannot foresee which stations will be broadcasting on what frequencies, let alone what those stations will be transmitting. At a later date, in *Radio Music* (1956), he could dispense with detailed instructions and simply offer a piece 'for one to eight performers, each at one radio'. Again, there is no intention to produce a work: 'having written radio music', Cage notes, 'has enabled me to accept not only the sounds I there encounter [in Times Square], but the television, radio and Muzak ones which nearly constantly and everywhere offer them-selves. . . . I am more and more realizing, that is to say, that I have ears and can hear. My work is intended as a demonstration of this; you might call it an affirmation of life.'

The mid-sixties, the great age of 'happenings', found Cage instigating similar demonstrations on a larger scale. Grandest of all was the 'Musicircus' of 1967 for which Cage assembled numerous composers and performers, two jazz bands, light shows, refresh-ment stalls, large balloons and an audience. His published pieces of the same period include *Variations IV* (1963), 'for any number of players, any sounds or combinations of sounds produced by any means, with or without other activities', and the more structured *HPSCHD* (1967–9), which presents notated material for from one to seven amplified harpsichords, together with from one to fifty-one pre-recorded tape tracks. Both these pieces have been recorded, which obviously gives them a quite alien fixedness, even a classic status, but the spirit of confusion is happily not lost. The recordings of *Variations IV* provide a bewildering sweep of sound detritus, a vast expansion from *Williams Mix*, while that of *HPSCHD* has instructions for the listener to keep varying playback controls.

All these pieces by Cage, it should be clear, cannot offer, and are not meant to offer, an auditory experience of any great significance. Their function is, rather, educational, in that they can serve to make the hearer aware of his sound environment, and for Cage this is perhaps the only intention. 'If you want to know the truth of the matter', Cage has said, 'the music I prefer, even to my own or anybody else's, is what we are hearing if we are just quiet.'

It is ironic that, despite Cage's avowed preference, his work has had a great influence on the aims and attitudes of other composers. Not only did he lay the foundations of live electronic music, as discussed in the last chapter, but he has also stimulated others to work with collage and mixed media. A great deal of his output could be described as exemplifying the latter, since there is often, as in *Cartridge Music*, an essential visual, even theatrical element. But the term 'mixed media' would normally be reserved for such jamborees as *Variations IV* or else for pieces like the two short items which Cage composed for Italian television in 1958, *Sounds of Venice* and *Water Walk*, both designed for solo performance by the composer using a variety of sound-producing means.

These pieces are among the very few musical works expressly designed for television or film. With the exception of the West-deutscher Rundfunk, who have presented audio-visual compositions such as Jan W. Morthenson's *Supersonics* (1970) and Bernard Parmegiani's *Das Auge hört – L'écran transparent* (1973, created in collaboration with Salvador Dali), broadcasting authorities have been less generous with television than with radio faċilities. And yet, as the works of Morthenson and of the Whitney brothers demonstrate, the combination of electronic sound with abstract images holds exciting possibilities. John Whitney has pointed out that electronic sound comes without any visual connotations (of instruments or of musicians performing) and so without any hindrance to its being experienced in parallel with freely invented film. Moreover, cinematic images might provide that visual focus whose absence appears to be detrimental to the success of much tape music.

Varèse intended that his *Déserts* for orchestra and tape should be accompanied by a film (it was to be that way round), and though the project came to nothing, his ideas are of interest. He insisted that the film should be 'purely of light phenomena', without action or narrative: 'The film must be absolutely in opposition with the score. Only opposition enables one to avoid paraphrase. Certain violent moments in the music must be accompanied by antagonizing images. . . . Voices, and hence dialogue, will be avoided. There will be no mixture of the human, vocal element with the organized sound and the instrumental ensemble.'

If the development of abstract sound-film combinations has been slow, more has been achieved with presentations of a 'son et lumière' character. Several electronic works, such as Pousseur's *Trois visages de Liège*, have been commissioned for entertainments of this character, though in Pousseur's case music by Gershwin was used instead. Xenakis has created works of tape sound and laser light, both devised by himself, and Henry had worked on several occasions with the light artist Nicolas Schöffer. Their theatre piece *Kyldex I* (1973), done in collaboration also with the choreographer Alwin Nikolais, brought together electronic music, light show and abstract dance; the title is an acronym for 'kybernetisch-lumino-dynamisches Experiment'.

Nikolais's ballets, or 'sound and vision pieces' as he prefers to call them, more usually have electronic accompaniments of his own composition, and he has normally taken charge also of lighting and design with the aim of producing a play of shape and colour rather than of characters or human forms. Such endeavours can be traced back to the work of Oskar Schlemmer at the Bauhaus in the twenties, and in particular to his *Triadic Ballet* (1922), so called because it was in three parts and required three dancers in abstract, figure-disguising costumes. Schlemmer was interested in the development of electronic music as a natural counterpart to non-narrative dance, but the *Triadic Ballet* was eventually performed to a Hindemith score for mechanical organ.

Another choreographer, Merce Cunningham, has been closely associated with Cage and other composers of the American avant-garde, and has played a notable part in the more recent evolution of mixed-media art. Especially interesting in the present connection was his role in Cage's *Variations V* (1965), for which Tudor and Mumma prepared complex circuitry to derive sounds directly from the dancers' movements. Sensitive antennae were used, as in the theremin, together with light beams falling on photocells, as in burglar alarms; the dancers, moving towards or away from the antennae and interrupting the light beams, triggered the release of sounds from tape recorders, record players and radios. As in *HPSCHD* there were also films and slides contributing to what Mumma called 'a superbly poly: -chromatic, -genic, -phonic, -meric, -morphic, -pagic, -technic, -valent, multi-ringed circus'.

Other composers of mixed-media events have not shared Cage's delight in multiple focus but instead have used the resources of music (electronic, vocal and instrumental), language, gesture, lighting and so on to serve a more or less clear dramatic idea. Among American composers, Salvatore Martirano, Roger Reynolds and Eric Salzman have been particularly active in this field, and Martirano's *L's GA* (1967–8) can stand as example. This is a setting of Lincoln's Gettysburg Address (hence the title) for 'gas-masked politico' – an actor inhaling helium to raise his voice to a thin squeak – with films and loud electronic music, the whole converting the great monument of American oratory into a grotesque rant.

Much is lost, of course, when such works are recorded, and some composers have preferred to regard recordings of their mixed-media compositions as entirely distinct pieces. For example, Reynolds's *Ping* (1968) is in its original version a dramatic work based on Beckett's prose piece, with the text projected by means of slides and accompanied by music and dance or film; but the recording is a purely musical work for flute, piano, harmonium and percussion, the instrumental sounds being interestingly ring modulated with each other and heard above material on tape.

A less drastic depletion of resources from live to recorded version occurs in the case of Salzman's *Nude Paper Sermon* for actor, Renaissance consort, chorus, electronics and tape (1968–9). The record, mixed in the studio, is something quite different from a live performance, but the stylistic heterogeneity and the deliberate inconsequentiality of the original are maintained. The sermon leads a circuitous path through assortments of speech, song and instrumental playing, including a madrigal set in pastiche sixteenth-century style as a 'ruin'. The man-centred sensibility of the Renaissance, it is suggested, has given way to new modes of thought without any such fixed poles. 'Electronic technology', Salzman has written of the piece, 'is used not only to provide new layers and new kinds of sound but also to project sound throughout the entire performer–audience space, to relate live, amplified and pre-recorded sound, and to interrelate a variety of electronic-age experiences. This interplay of styles – of "ways of life" – helps integrate purely musical (or aural) structures and the other elements of the total experience and provides the basis for a truly contemporary theater.'

However, a 'truly contemporary theater' is not to be achieved merely by the introduction of electronics, and much mixed-media work appears to be based on the quite unjustified assumption that musical sophistication (at least in the technology employed) can be matched with dramatic ineptitude. The theatre and film works of Kagel, by contrast, show what can be accomplished when a composer has as much dramatic as musical flair. His *Tremens* (1963–5), described as the 'scenic montage of a medical test', is a one-act play for which Kagel wrote the text, composed the music and devised the hospital setting. Like much of Kagel's work *Tremens* is an amused satire on aspects of western musical life: in a bizarre reversal of music therapy, music is seen as an insidious influence and the instrumentalists are discovered in curtained cubicles on stage.

Stockhausen's *Alphabet für Liège* (1972) could be considered a benign counterweight to Kagel's piece, for here the composer extols the power of musical vibration over animate and inanimate objects. The work is a sort of exhibition, at which the several stands all have something to demonstrate about the physical or mystical force of electronic, vocal or instrumental sound. A visitor may find a singer using mantras to affect different parts of the body, or other musicians showing how sounds can set up patterns in water or powder, or still others using vibrations to alter the gill movements of fish. The tone of the exhibition is one of intellectual curiosity but also one of serious, almost ritualized exploration. 'Originally with church and tribal music', Stockhausen has said, 'the making of the sound itself brought you into the state of trance and meditation, adoration or ecstasy. This has disappeared, and all we have now is the more or less mocking attitude of a concertgoer or someone with his radio or tape recorder who uses music as an acoustical tapestry or, at best, something to identify with, a particular emotion that's dominating him at the moment. But a new function of sounds, of certain constellations of sounds composed by persons who had this more subtle knowledge of what sounds do to man, might suggest records made for very particular purposes.'

The idea proposed here and in *Alphabet*, of using sound to achieve quite defined effects on the psyche, is an ancient one, long acknowledged in the Indian use of mantras and ragas for specific purposes. In western society, however, it has become a subject of interest only since the arrival of electronic means, which can demonstrate psychic and physiological effects of sound in a relatively gross manner. At the most trivial level, the productive effects of 'music while you work' and the relaxation induced by 'muzak' have been recognized for many years, but only since the late sixties have there been attempts to use sound environments more subtly. The record series with the title *Environments*, for instance, offers recordings from nature to be used as aural backgrounds in the home.

Among composers, LaMonte Young was perhaps the first to see the possibilities here, influenced, like Stockhausen, by eastern uses of music. 'I maintained an environment of constant periodic sound waveforms', he has written, 'almost continuously from September 1966 through January 1970. . . . the sets of frequency ratios were often played continuously 24 hours a day for several weeks or months at a stretch. Marian and I sang, worked and lived in this environment and studied its effects on ourselves and the varied groups of people who were invited to spend time with the frequencies.' Similar environments have been set up by Young and his colleagues, though for shorter periods, at universities, art galleries and festivals, creating what he refers to as 'Dream Houses'. 'The work presented within these model Dream Houses', he goes on, 'consists of a total environmental set of frequency structures in the media of sound and light. Two sources are used to produce the frequencies in the sound medium: the sine wave oscillators generate a continuous live electronic sound environment, and The Theatre of Eternal Music [Young's performing ensemble] performs additional frequencies at prescribed time intervals.' Young's eventual aim is the foundation of permanent Dream Houses where the euphony of pure sine waves in exact frequency ratios, joined by chant and solemn instrumental contribution, may play on without interruption.

Electronic music does indeed seem best suited to the kind of auditorium in which an audience would be free to enter and leave as they pleased, to sit or to wander at will. Stockhausen had the chance to work in such an environment at Expo 70 in Osaka, where a specially designed music dome was erected for continuous programmes of his tape and live electronic music. Moreover, the very design of such works as *Alphabet* and *Sternklang* presumes that the audience will move within the performing area, while in many of his works since *Kontakte* Stockhausen has used 'moment form', in which, theoretically, it does not matter if the listener misses some moments through inattention or absence. In fact it does matter, for even in his most relaxedly environmental works, such as the four-hour *Ensemble* (1967) which had compositions by twelve students being played together in a large assembly hall, he insists on a detailed 'form scheme', and he has never followed his American contemporaries in abandoning the notion of the composed work.

The difference between Stockhausen and Cage, in particular, becomes evident when one examines their respective collage techniques, their opposed responses to the stream of electronic consciousness. Where Cage, in such works as *Fontana Mix*, is at pains to impose no order on his material, Stockhausen's aim is always the creation of unity from diversity, and he declares that the term 'collage' cannot be applied to his work, where the central idea is that of mediation between extremes. His tape piece *Telemusik* (1966) exemplifies this. Composed during a visit to Japan, the work uses the sounds of Japanese temple instruments – bells and woodblocks – to define the starting points of its thirty-two sections, but references to alien cultures do not end there. Much of the piece is created from recordings of the world's music, including Japanese gagaku, Balinese gamelan playing, Hungarian folk music, song from the southern Sahara and so on. These raw materials are usually combined with each other, and so rendered more or less unrecognizable, by the technique of 'intermodulation', projecting, that is, a parameter from one recording onto another. 'I modulate the rhythm of one event', Stockhausen explains, 'with the dynamic curve of another. Or I modulate electronic chords, regulated by myself, with the dynamic curve of a priestly chant, then this with the monotonous song (thus the pitch line) of a Shipibo song, and so on.'

Intermodulation produces complex textures and events in which the original recording, when it can be distinguished at all, sounds as if it is being jammed by radio interference. This, coupled with Stockhausen's use of twittering high frequency tones throughout much of *Telemusik*, gives the work something of the character of a shortwave reception, a result which perhaps contributed to Stockhausen's later use of shortwave radios in *Kurzwellen* and other works. But, unlike those Cage pieces which use radios or the imagery of radio, *Telemusik* and *Kurzwellen* are purposefully constructed by means of techniques on integration. Stockhausen has described *Telemusik* as 'a universality of past, present and future, of distant places and spaces', but it is also quite definitely a work by Stockhausen, a work which fuses exotic presences into the ringing high-register continuum of the earlier *Studie II*, and a work whose soaring sounds might almost have escaped from *Kontakte*.

Stockhausen pursued his aim for a 'music of the whole world' in his next tape piece, *Hymnen* (1966–7), a piece which is in every respect more open than *Telemusik*. It lasts for almost two hours, by comparison with the $17\frac{1}{2}$ minutes of the earlier work, and its source material, the national anthems of the world, gains free acknowledgment in a great festival of quotation. There is also now a stronger feeling of broadcast reception: the well-fashioned scheme of *Telemusik* is replaced by an allusive drift of thought and sometimes, as in one section ominously punctuated by the calls of a croupier, of dream. Furthermore, according to the composer: 'The work is composed in such a way that different libretti or scenarios for films, operas, and ballets can be compiled for this music. The arrangement of the individual parts and the total duration are variable. Regions [Stockhausen uses this word for the work's four large sections] can be interchanged – depending on dramatic requirements – extended or omitted.' Stockhausen himself has prepared versions of the work with live electronic ensemble participating throughout, imitating what they hear and forging new connections between events on tape, and also with orchestra playing in the third region.

Although Stockhausen has again insisted that *Hymnen* is 'not a collage' – and indeed the techniques of intermodulation are again used to effect mediations – it is hard to avoid taking the anthems at face value and interpreting the work as a plea for, or perhaps a promise of, universal brotherhood. Indeed, the composer invites one to do this by giving the fourth and final region a centre in an invented anthem 'associated with the Utopian realm of Hymnunion in Harmondie under Pluramon'. As Karl H. Wörner has pointed out, this imaginary country contains in its name a play on 'hymn union', 'harmonia mundi' and 'pluralism monism', as if Stockhausen were suggesting that national rivalries may be forgotten in an awareness that the variety of mankind does not conflict with a higher unity. For each human being contains the potential to be a Spaniard, a South American Indian, a Balinese or whatever, and through the music of other cultures, Stockhausen has said, we may find within ourselves the men of other times and places. The message of the electronic medium, finally, is not that we inhabit a global village but that the world inhabits each of us.

III Appendices

III.1 Recordings

A complete catalogue of recorded electronic music would make a considerably larger volume than this book. The following select list is arranged by composer, each entry giving the title of the work, its date and approximate duration, the musical forces required, the publisher of the score (if any) and the record number or numbers. Where a work has been recorded in different versions or performances the pertinent record numbers are separated by semicolons; division by commas is used for different issues of the same music. Twenty discs, their numbers marked with asterisks, have been chosen as providing a basic library representing electronic music in its diverse forms.

AMM (fl. London, 1965–9). Group of improvisers using electronic and conventional instruments.

Improvisation (1968, 23½′). Mainstream MS 5002

Arel, Bülent (b. Istanbul, 1919). Resident in the USA since 1959, composing most of his electronic music at the Columbia–Princeton Center in New York. His works show a flamboyant and assured handling of classic studio techniques in the manipulation of synthetic sounds.

Dramatic Fragment from 'The Scapegoat' (1961, 1½′), tape. Son Nova S 3

Electronic Music no. 1 (1960, 8½′), tape. CRI S 356, Son Nova S 3

Mimiana II: Frieze (1969, 13′), tape. CRI SD 300

Sacred Service: Prelude and Postlude (1961, 7′), tape. CRI S 356, Son Nova S 3

Stereo Electronic Music no. 1 (1960, 10½′), tape. Columbia MS 6566

Stereo Electronic Music no. 2 (1970, 14½′), tape. *CRI SD 268, Finnadar 9010 Q

Ashley, Robert (b. Ann Arbor, Mich., 1930). Co-founder of the Cooperative Studio for Electronic Music in Ann Arbor (1958) and member of the Sonic Arts Union, performing live electronic music since 1966. A leading figure in the experimental wing of American music, he has used a wide variety of electronic means in the creation of what is often bizarre sound-imagery.

Purposeful Lady Slow Afternoon (1968), electronic music theatre. *Mainstream MS 5010

Untitled Mixes (1965, 5'), jazz trio + tape. ESP 1009

The Wolfman (1964, 6'), amplified voice + tape (*Source* magazine no. 4). ESP 1009; Source 1

Babbitt, Milton (b. Philadelphia, Pa, 1916). Prominent as composer and theorist in the development of twelve-note serialism along rigorous lines. In his electronic music he has worked exclusively with the RCA Synthesizer at the Columbia–Princeton Center in New York.

Composition for Synthesizer (1960–61, 10½'), tape. Columbia MS 6566

Ensembles for Synthesizer (1962–4, 10½'), tape. *Columbia MS 7051, Finnadar 9010 Q

Philomel (1963, 19'), soprano + tape (Associated). Acoustic Research AR 0654 083

Phonemena (1969–74, 4'), soprano + tape (Peters). New World NW 209

Reflections (1974–5, 10'), piano + tape (Peters). New World NW 209

Vision and Prayer (1961, 14½'), soprano + tape (Associated). *CRI SD 268

Badings, Henk (b. Bandung, Indonesia, 1907). Dutch pioneer of tape music, bringing a neo-classical style to the medium.

Capriccio (1959, 7½'), violin + tape (Donemus). Epic BC 1118, Philips 835 056 AY, Philips SABL 206

Evolutionen (1957, 14'), tape. Epic BC 1118, Philips 835 056 AY, Philips SABL 206

Genese (1958, 15'), tape. Epic BC 1118, Philips 835 056 AY, Philips SABL 206

Kaïn en Abel (1956, 17½'), tape. Philips 400 036 AE, Philips ABE 10073

Barraqué, Jean (b. Paris, 1928; d. Paris, 1973). Known chiefly for his small output of grandly imposing works for conventional forces, but also composed one electronic piece.

Etude (1953, 4′), tape. Barclay 89005

Bayle, François (b. Tamatava, Madagascar, 1932). Member of the Groupe de Recherches Musicales (Paris) since 1961 and latterly director. His works use *musique concrète* techniques with unusual sensitivity.

Archipel (1963, 7–18′), string quartet + tape. Philips 836 895 DSY

Espaces inhabitables (1966–7, 18′), tape. Philips 836 895 DSY

Jeîta, ou Murmure des eaux (1970), tape. Philips 6521 016

Lignes et points (1966, 7′), tape. Philips 836 895 DSY

L'oiseau chanteur (1964, 4′), tape. Candide CE 31025, Philips 836 895 DSY, *Varèse VS 81005

Pluriel (1962–3, 8′), seventeen instruments + tape. Philips 836 894 DSY

Solitioude, tape. Philips 6740 001

Vapeur (1963, 5′), tape. Boîte à Musique LD 072

Behrman, David (b. Salzburg, 1937). Member of the Sonic Arts Union, performing live electronic music since 1966.

Runthrough (1966, 15′), live electronic ensemble + tape. *Mainstream MS 5010

Wave Train (1967, 12–18′), live electronic ensemble (*Source* magazine no. 3). Source 1

Berio, Luciano (b. Oneglia, 1925). Pioneer of electronic and avant-garde music in Italy; co-founder with Bruno Maderna of the Studio di Fonologia Musicale in Milan in 1955.

Différences (1958, 17′), five instruments + tape. Mainstream MS 5004; Philips 839 323 DSY, Philips 6500 631

Momenti (1957, 7′), tape. Limelight LS 86047, Philips 836 897 DSY, Philips 835 485 AY

Perspectives (1957, 7′), tape. Compagnia Generale del Disco ESZ 3

Thema – omaggio a Joyce (1958, 6½′), tape. Philips 836 897 DSY, Philips 835 485 AY, Turnabout TV 34177 S

Visage (1961, 21'), tape. Candide CE 31027, Columbia OS 3320, RCA 61079, *Turnabout TV 34046 S

Birtwistle, Harrison (b. Accrington, 1934). Has worked much more with conventional forces than with electronics, but brings to both media a concern with time and continuous, organic development.
Chronometer (1971, 24'), tape. Argo ZRG 790
Four Interludes from a Tragedy (1970, 7½'), clarinet + tape. L'Oiseau-Lyre DSLO 17

Boretz, Benjamin (b. Brooklyn, NY, 1934). Follows Babbitt in his elaborately worked serial compositions, including the computer-synthesized piece below.
Group Variations (1969–73, 12'), tape. CRI SD 300

Boucourechliev, André (b. Sofia, 1925). Best known for aleatory instrumental scores on the Boulezian model, but briefly associated with studios in Paris and Milan.
Texte I (1958, 6½'), tape. Philips 835 486 AY
Texte II (1959, 5'), tape. Boîte à Musique LD 071

Boulez, Pierre (b. Montbrison, 1925). Leader of the avant-garde since his first works appeared in the late forties. He worked with electronics only intermittently before becoming, in 1977, director of the Institut de Recherche et Coordination Acoustique/Musique, Paris.
Etude II (1952, 3'), tape. Barclay 89005

Brown, Earle (b. Lunenburg, Mass., 1926). Associated with John Cage in the early fifties, but his later works show a kinship rather with the European avant-garde.
Four Systems (1954), graphic score. EMI Electrola C 065 02469 (live electronic version)
Times Five (1963, 15½'), five instruments + tape (Universal). Boîte à Musique LD 072

Cage, John (b. Los Angeles, Calif., 1912). Has had a major influence on younger composers since the second world war, particularly through his invoking of chance in composition. He also initiated live electronic music and has worked extensively in this medium, often with a bewildering plurality of resources.

Cartridge Music (1960), amplified sounds (Peters). Mainstream MS 5015, Time S 8009; DGG 137 009

Credo in Us (1942, 12'), percussion quartet including gramophone or radio (Peters). EMI Electrola C 165 28954

Fontana Mix (1958, up to 17'), tape (Peters). *Turnabout TV 34046 S; Mainstream MS 5005, Time S 8003 (with *Aria*); Columbia MS 7139 (live electronic percussion version)

HPSCHD (1967–9), harpsichords + tapes. Nonesuch H 71224

Imaginary Landscape no. 1 (1939, 6'), electronic devices + percussion + piano (Peters). Avakian JCS 1; EMI Electrola C 165 28954

Music for Amplified Toy Pianos (1960, 12') (Peters). Cramps CRS LP 6101; EMI Electrola C 065 02469

Radio Music (1956, 6'), up to eight performers at radios (Peters). Cramps CRS LP 6101

Rozart Mix (1965), tape loops (Peters). EMI Electrola C 165 28954

Sixty-Two Mesostics re Merce Cunningham (1971), amplified voice (Peters). Cramps CRS LP 6101 (extracts)

Solos for Voice 2 (1960) (Peters). Odyssey 32 16 0156 (electronic choral version)

Variations II (1961), variable forces (Peters). *Columbia MS 7051 (amplified piano version)

Variations IV (1963), variable forces (Peters). Everest 3132; Everest 3230 (both made up of extracts from a performance using diverse electronic equipment)

Williams Mix (1951–2), tape. Avakian JCS 1

Carlos, Walter (b. Pawtucket, RI, 1939). His Bach arrangements made 'Moog' a household word, but he has also composed original electronic works.

Dialogues (1963, 4'), piano +tape. Turnabout TV 34004 S

Sonic Seasonings (1971–2), tape. Columbia PG 31234

Switched on Bach (1968), tape. Columbia MS 7194

Variations (1964, 4'), flute + tape. Turnabout TV 34004 S

The Well-Tempered Synthesizer (1969), tape. Columbia MS 7286

Davidovsky, Mario (b. Buenos Aires, 1934). Resident in the USA since 1960, producing his electronic works at the Columbia–Princeton Center in New York. He uses classic studio techniques to generate strong musical gestures.

Electronic Study no. 1 (1960, 6′), tape. Columbia MS 6566
Electronic Study no. 2 (1962, 6½′), tape. CRI S 356, Son Nova S 3
Electronic Study no. 3 (1965–6, 5′), tape. Finnadar 9010 Q, Turnabout TV 34487 S
Synchronisms no. 1 (1963, 4½′), flute + tape (McGinnis & Marx). CRI SD 204
Synchronisms no. 2 (1964, 6′), four instruments + tape (McGinnis & Marx). CRI SD 204
Synchronisms no. 3 (1964–5, 5′), cello + tape. (McGinnis & Marx. CRI SD 204
Synchronisms no. 5 (1970, 8½′), five percussion + tape. *CRI SD 268; Turnabout TV 34487 S
Synchronisms no. 6 (1970), piano + tape. Turnabout TV 34487 S

Dodge, Charles (b. Ames, Iowa, 1942). One of the foremost composers working with computer sound synthesis.

Changes (1970, 15½′), tape. *Nonesuch H 71245
Earth's Magnetic Field (1970, 29½′), tape. Nonesuch H 71250
Extensions (1973, 8′), trumpet + tape. CRI SD 300
In Celebration (1975, 8½′), tape. CRI SD 348
Speech Songs (1973, 7′), tape. CRI SD 348
The Story of Our Lives (1974, 18½′), tape. CRI SD 348

Druckman, Jacob (b. Philadelphia, Pa, 1928). Has used tape as an adjunct in pieces exploiting performers' virtuosity.

Animus I (1966, 12½′), trombone + tape. Turnabout TV 34177 S
Animus II (1967), mezzo + two percussion + tape. CRI SD 255
Animus III (1969, 15½′), clarinet + tape. Nonesuch H 71253
Synapse → Valentine (1970, 18½′), double bass + tape. Nonesuch H 71253

Eaton, John (b. Bryn Mawr, Pa, 1935). Developed, with Paul Ketoff, the synket as a synthesizer for live performance, and has used it in a series of highly charged scores.

Blind Man's Cry (1968, 11′), soprano + synthesizers. CRI SD 296
Concert Piece (1967), synket + orchestra. Turnabout TV 34428 S
Duet for Synket and Moog (1968). Decca 710165
Mass (1970, 20′), soprano + clarinet + synthesizers + tape. CRI SD 296

Piece for Solo Synket no. 3 (1966). Decca 710154
Soliloquy (1967), synket. Decca 710165
Song for R.P.B. (1964), soprano + synket (Shawnee). Decca 710154
Thoughts on Rilke (1967), soprano + synket. Decca 710165

Eimert, Herbert (b. Bad Kreuznach, 1897; d. Cologne, 1972). Founder director of the Studio für Elektronische Musik at the Cologne radio station (1953), where he created some of the first electronically generated tape pieces.

Epitaph für Aikichi Kuboyama (1960–62, 23½') tape. Wergo 60014
Etüde über Tongemische (1953–4, 4'), tape. DGG LP 16132
Fünf Stücke (1955–6, 13'), tape. DGG LP 16132
Glockenspiel (1953, 1'), tape. DGG LP 16132
Sechs Studien (1962, 18'), tape. Wergo 60014
Selektion I (1959–60, 10'), tape. Philips 835 486 AY
Variante einer Variation von Anton Webern (1958, 1'), tape. Wergo 60006
Zu Ehren von Igor Stravinsky (1957, 1'), tape. Wergo 60006

Ferrari, Luc (b. Paris, 1929). Worked with the Groupe de Recherches Musicales in Paris (1958–66). Composer of *musique concrète*, of aural collage (*Hétérozygote*) and of environment recordings (*Presque rien* series).

Composé-composite (1962–3, 9'), instruments + tape. Philips 836 894 DSY
Etude aux accidents (1958, 2'), tape. Boîte à Musique LD 070
Etude aux sons tendus (1958, 3'), tape. Boîte à Musique LD 070
Hétérozygote (1963–4, 27'), tape. Philips 836 885 DSY
J'ai été coupé (1969), tape. Philips 836 885 DSY
Music Promenade (1964–9), four tape recorders. Wergo 60046
Presque rien no. 1 (1970), tape. DGG 2543 004
Tautologos I (1961, 4½'), tape. Boîte à Musique LD 072
Tautologos II (1961, 15'), tape. Boîte à Musique LD 072
Tête et queue du dragon (1959–60, 9'), tape. Candide CE 31025, Philips 835 487 AY, *Varèse VS 81005
Und so weiter (1966, 12'), piano + tape. Wergo 60046
Visage V (1958–9, 10½'), tape. Limelight LS 86047, Philips 835 485 AY, Philips 6740 001

Gaburo, Kenneth (b. Somerville, NJ, 1926). Has used various electronic techniques in exploring music-language correspondences.

Antiphony III (Pearl-White Moments) (1962, 16½'), chorus + tape. Nonesuch H 71199

Antiphony IV (Poised) (1967, 9½'), voice + three instruments + live electronics. Nonesuch H 71199

Exit Music I: The Wasting of Lucrecetzia (1964, 3½'), tape. Nonesuch H 71199

Exit Music II: Fat Millie's Lament (1965, 4½'), tape. Nonesuch H 71199

For Harry (1966, 5'), tape. CRI S 356, Heliodor HS 25047

Lemon Drops (1965, 3'), tape. CRI S 356, Heliodor HS 25047

Gerhard, Roberto (b. Valls, Catalonia, 1896; d. Cambridge, 1970). Resident in England from the early thirties, he worked with his own equipment and at the BBC Radiophonic Workshop.

Symphony no. 3 'Collages' (1960, 19'), orchestra + tape. Angel S 36558

Glass, Philip (b. Baltimore, Md, 1937). Has worked since the late sixties with his own ensemble of electronic and amplified instruments, playing music based on repetition, regularity and glowing tonal harmony.

Contrary Motion (1969, 15½'), electric organ. Shandar 83 515

Music in Fifths (1969, 23'), two soprano saxophones + electric organ. Chatham Sq LP 1003

Music in Similar Motion (1969, 17'), three woodwind + three electric organs. Chatham Sq LP 1003

North Star (1977, 34½'), voices + instruments + electric instruments. Virgin V 2085

Two Pages (1969, 17'), electric organ + piano. Folkways 33902; Shandar 83 515

Hambraeus, Bengt (b. Stockholm, 1928). Swedish pioneer of electronic music, working mostly with recordings of conventional instruments.

Konstellationer II (1959, 16'), tape (Nordiska). Philips 838 750 AY

Rota II (1963, 12'), tape. Riks Lp 7 s
Tetragon (1965, 18'), tape. Riks Lp 7 s

Henry, Pierre (b. Paris, 1927). Collaborated with Pierre Schaeffer in the Paris *musique concrète* studio from 1949, then in 1958 left to found his own Studio Apsome in Paris. His large output includes music for ballets, films and stage plays as well as concert works of many kinds.

Antiphonie (1952, 3'), tape. Ducretet-Thomson DUC 9, London DTL 93121

Apocalypse de Jean (1968), tape. Philips C 3017, Philips 6521 001–3

Astrologie (1953, 7½'), tape. Ducretet-Thomson DUC 9, London DTL 93121

Batterie fugace (1950–51, 2½'), tape. Ducretet-Thomson DUC 8, London DTL 93090

Ceremony (1969), tape. Philips 849 512

Concerto des ambiguïtés (1950, 34'), tape. Philips 6510 012; Ducretet-Thomson DUC 8, London DTL 93090 (finale only)

Cortical Art III (1973), tape. Philips 6510 015

Entité (1960, 6'), tape. Limelight LS 86048, Philips 835 486 AY, Philips 836 887 DSY

Granulométrie (1962–7), tape. Philips 836 892 DSY

Machine Dance (1973), tape. Philips 6510 013

Maléfices (1961, 33'), tape. Philips 432 762 BE

Mise en musique du corticalart (1971), tape. Philips 6521 022

Mouvement-rythme-étude (1970), tape. Philips 6504 052

Messe de Liverpool (1967), tape. Philips 6501 0001

Messe pour le temps présent (1970), tape. Philips 836 893 DSY; *Philips 6510 014 (extract)

Musique sans titre (1950–51, 25'), tape. Ducretet-Thomson DUC 8, London DTL 93090 (extracts)

Musiques pour une fête (1971) , tape. Philips 6565 001

La noire à soixante (1961, 23½'), tape. Philips 836 892 DSY

Orphée (1958, 120'), tape. Philips 839 484 LY

Prismes (1973), tape. Philips 6510 016

La reine verte (1963, 53'), tape. Philips 6332 015, Unidisc STE 30 300 s; *Philips 6510 014, Philips 836 893 DSY (extract)

Spirale, tape. Philips 836 887 DSY

Tam-tam III (1950–51, 4′), tape. Ducretet-Thomson DUC 8, London DTL 93090

Tam-tam IV (1950–51, 3½′), tape. Ducretet-Thomson DUC 9, London DTL 93121

Variations pour une porte et un soupir (1963, 54½′), tape. Philips 836 898 DSY; *Philips 6510 014 (extract)

Vocalises (1952, 3′), tape. Ducretet-Thomson DUC 9, London DTL 93121

Le voile d'Orphée (1953, 15½′), tape. Ducretet-Thomson DUC 8, London DTL 93090, Philips 836 887 DSY , Supraphon DV 6221

Le voyage (1962, 53′), tape. Limelight LS 86049, Philips 836 899 DSY; *Philips 6510 014 (extract)

——with Pierre Schaeffer

Bidule en ut (1950, 2½′), tape. Ducretet-Thomson DUC 8, London DTL 93090, Philips 6736 006

Symphonie pour un homme seul (1949–50, 22′), disc. Ducretet-Thomson DUC 9, London DTL 93121

Henze, Hans Werner (b. Gütersloh, Westphalia, 1926). Leading composer of operas and of works inspired by socialist revolutionary politics. Has occasionally used tapes in works for conventional media.

Tristan (1973, 43½′), piano + orchestra + tape. DGG 2530 834

Violin Concerto no. 2 (1971, 25′), violin + orchestra + tape. Decca Headline HEAD 5

Hiller, Lejaren (b. New York, NY 1924). Founder director of the experimental studio at the University of Illinois (1958–68), where he developed computer programmes for composition.

Algorithms I (1968), nine instruments + tape. DGG 2543 005

An Avalanche (1968), performers + tape (Presser). Heliodor HS 2549 006

Computer Cantata (1963, 24′), soprano + instruments + tape (Presser). CRI SD 310

Computer Music (1968), percussion + tape. Heliodor HS 2549 006

Machine Music (1964, 13′), piano + percussion + tape (Presser). Heliodor HS 25047

Nightmare Music from 'Time of the Heathen' (1961, 10′), tape.

Heliodor HS 2549 006

Peroration (1962–3, 5½′), tape. Jornadas de Musica Experimental JME ME I

Suite (1966, 18′), two pianos + tape. Heliodor HS 2549 006

Vocalise (1962–3, 5½′), tape. Supraphon DV 6221

Holliger, Heinz (b. Langenthal, Switzerland, 1939). Composer and oboist who has used electronics to extend instrumental capabilities.

Siebengesang (1967), oboe + orchestra + voices + electronics. DGG 2530 318

Kagel, Mauricio (b. Buenos Aires, 1932). Resident in Cologne since 1957, working at the studio there and with his own performing group. His pieces often use unusual techniques and sound-producing devices.

Acustica (1968–70, 25′), instruments + electronics. DGG 2707 059

Transición I (1958–60, 13′), tape. Limelight LS 86048, Philips 835 486 AY

Transición II (1958–9, 8–24′), two players at a piano + two tape recorders (Universal). Mainstream MS 5003, Time S 8001

Unter Strom (1969, 22–30′), three players + electronics. DGG 2530 460

Koenig, Gottfried Michael (b. Magdeburg, 1926). Worked with Stockhausen and others at the Cologne studio (1954–64) and then became artistic director of the studio at Utrecht University, where he has worked on computer sound synthesis.

Funktion Blau (1969), tape. Philips 6736 006, Philips 6740 002

Funktion Gelb (1968), tape. Wergo 324

Funktion Grün (1967), tape. DGG 137 011

Klangfiguren II (1955–6, 10½′), tape. DGG LP 16134

Terminus II (1966–7, 19′), tape. DGG 137 011

Terminus X (1967), tape. Philips 836 993 DSY

Krenek, Ernst (b. Vienna, 1900). Has maintained an inquisitive interest in new techniques throughout his creative life. He was one of the earliest visitors to the Cologne studio, where he produced his *Pfingstoratorium*.

Pfingstoratorium–Spiritus intelligentiae, sanctus (1956, 17'),
tape. DGG LP 16134
Quintona (1965, 9'), tape. Jornadas de Musica Experimental JME
ME 2

Lansky, Paul (b. New York, NY, 1944). Influenced by George
Perle's twelve-tone modality and by developments in computer
sound synthesis at Princeton University.
mild und leise (1973–4, 18½'), tape. Odyssey Y 34139

Le Caine, Hugh (b. Port Arthur, Ontario, 1914). Active in electronic music as composer and instrument-builder since the thirties.
Dripsody (1955, 2'), tape. Folkways 33436

Ligeti, György (b. Diciosanmartin, Transylvania, 1923). Moved to
Vienna in 1956 and worked at the Cologne studio in 1957–8. His
electronic pieces, like his more abundant works for live performers,
show richly worked textures and an unusual touch of wit.
Artikulation (1958, 4'), tape (Schott). Limelight LS 86048,
Philips 835 486 AY, Schott (with score), Wergo 60059
Glissandi (1957, 7½'), tape. Wergo 60076

Lucier, Alvin (b. Nashua, NH, 1931). Director of the studio at
Brandeis University (1961–9) and member of the Sonic Arts Union
performing live electronic music since 1966.
I am sitting in a room (1970), tape + slides (*Source* magazine
no. 7). Source 3
North American Time Capsule (1967), voices + electronics.
Odyssey 32 16 0156
Vespers(1968), performers with echo-location devices (*Source*
magazine no. 7). *Mainstream MS 5010

Luening, Otto (b. Milwaukee, Wisc., 1900). With Vladimir
Ussachevsky pioneered tape music in America in the early fifties;
since 1959 both composers have been associated with the Columbia–Princeton Center in New York. Luening has a characterful
neo-classical style.
Fantasy in Space (1952, 3'), tape. Desto DC 6466, Folkways FX
6160, Innovation GB 1
Gargoyles (1960, 8½'), violin + tape. Columbia MS 6566
In the Beginning (1956, 10'), tape. *CRI SD 268

Invention in Twelve Notes (1952, 3½'), tape. Desto DC 6466, Innovation GB I

Low Speed (1952, 3½'), tape. Desto DC 6466, Innovation GB I

Moonflight (1968), tape. Desto DC 6466

Synthesis (1962, 9'), orchestra + tape. CRI SD 219

——with Vladimir Ussachevsky

Carlsbad Caverns (1955, 1½'), tape. RCA Victor LPM 1280

Concerted Piece (1960, 9'), orchestra + tape. *CRI SD 227

Incantation (1953, 2½'), tape. Desto DC 6466, Innovation GB I

A Poem in Cycles and Bells (1954, 14'), orchestra + tape. CRI 112

Rhapsodic Variations (1953–4, 17'), orchestra + tape. Louisville 545 5

Suite from 'King Lear' (1956, 4½'), tape. CRI 112

Maderna, Bruno (b. Venice, 1920; d. Darmstadt, 1973). Prominent in avant-garde musical circles from the early fifties; co-founder with Luciano Berio of the Studio di Fonologia Musicale in Milan in 1955.

Continuo (1958, 8½'), tape. Limelight LS 86047, Philips 835 485 AY

Musica su due dimensioni (II) (1958, 11'), flute + tape (Suvini Zerboni). Compagnia Generale del Disco ESZ 3

Malec, Ivo (b. Zagreb, 1925). Resident from 1959 in Paris, where he has worked with the Groupe de Recherches Musicales. His tape pieces show a refined handling of *musique concrète*.

Cantate pour elle (1966, 14½'), soprano + harp + tape. Philips 836 891 DSY

Dahovi (1961, 6'), tape. Candide CE 31025, Philips 836 891 DSY, Philips 6740 001, *Varèse VS 81005

Reflets (1961, 2½'), tape. Boîte à Musique LD 072

Tutti (1962–3, 8½'), orchestra + tape. Philips 836 894 DSY

Messiaen, Olivier (b. Avignon, 1908). Used the ondes martenot in several scores of the thirties and forties; worked briefly at the Paris *musique concrète* studio in 1952.

Fête des belles eaux (1937), six ondes martenot. Erato STU 70102, Musical Heritage Society MHS 821

Mimaroglu, Ilhan (b. Istanbul, 1926). Resident in the USA since

1959. His fiercely dramatic electronic pieces make use of classic studio techniques.

Agony (1965, 9½'), tape. Finnadar 9012, *Turnabout TV 34046 S

Anacolutha: Encounter and Episode II (1965, 9'), tape. Finnadar SR 9001

Bowery Bum (1964, 3'), tape. Finnadar 9012, Turnabout TV 34004 S

Hyperboles (1971, 5'), tape. Finnadar SR 9001

Intermezzo (1964, 3'), tape. Finnadar 9012, Turnabout TV 34004 S

To Kill a Sunrise (1974), tape. Folkways 33951

Music for Jean Dubuffet's 'Coucou Bazar' (1973), tape. Finnadar SR 9003

Piano Music for Performer and Composer (1967), tape. Turnabout TV 34177 S

Preludes (1966–7), tape. Finnadar SR 9001 (no. 8); Finnadar 9012 (eight nos); Turnabout TB 34177 S (six nos)

Provocations (1971, 3'), tape. Finnadar SR 9001

La ruche, tape. Folkways 33951

Sing me a Song of Songmy (1970), tape. Atlantic SD 1576; Finnadar SR 9001 (extract)

Le tombeau d'Edgar Poe (1964), tape. Finnadar 9012, Turnabout TV 34004 S

Tract (1972–4), tape. Folkways 33441

White Cockatoo (1966, 4½'), tape. Finnadar SR 9001

Wings of the Delirious Demon (1969, 15'), tape. Finnadar SR 9001

Mumma, Gordon (b. Framingham, Mass., 1935). Co-founder of the Cooperative Studio for Electronic Music at Ann Arbor, Michigan (1958), and member of the Sonic Arts Union, performing live electronic music since 1966. Many works use specially constructed 'cybersonic' circuitry.

Cybersonic Cantilevers (1973), audience + electronics. Folkways FTS 33904

The Dresden Interleaf 13 February 1945 (1965, 14½'), tape. Jornadas de Musica Experimental JME ME 2

Hornpipe (1967), horn + electronics. *Mainstream MS 5010

Mesa (1965), bandoneon + electronics. Odyssey 32 16 0158

Music for the Venezia Space Theatre (1964, 12'), tape. Advance FGR 5

Peasant Boy (1965, 8½'), jazz trio + tape. ESP S 1009

Musica Elettronica Viva (fl. Rome, 1966–71). Live electronic ensemble of American composers and performers.

Spacecraft (1967, 20'), live electronic ensemble. Mainstream MS 5002

Nono, Luigi (b. Venice, 1924). Associated with Pierre Boulez and Karlheinz Stockhausen in the early fifties; subsequently allied himself more closely with the cause of socialism. He has worked since 1960 at the studio in Milan, often using tape in large-scale works for conventional forces.

Como una ola de fuerza y luz (1971–2, 30'), soprano + piano + orchestra + tape (Ricordi). DGG 2530 436

Contrappunto dialettico alla mente (1968), tape. DGG 2543 006

Y entonces comprendio (1969–70, 32'), voices + tape. DGG 2530 436, Ricordi SAVC 501

La fabbrica illuminata (1964, 14'), soprano + tape. *Wergo 60038

A floresta e jovem e cheja de vida (1966, 35'), performers + tape + electronics. Arcophon AC 6811, Musique Vivante HM 30767

Non consumiamo Marx (1969), voices + tape. I Dischi del Sole DS 182 4 CL

Omaggio a Vedova (1960, 5'), tape. Wergo 60067

Per Bastiana Tai-Yang Cheng (1967), orchestra + tape (Ricordi). Wergo 60067

Ricorda cosa ti hanno fatto in Auschwitz (1965, 11½'), soprano + children's chorus + tape. *Wergo 60038

Un volto, del mare (1969), voices + tape. I Dischi del Sole DS 182 4 CL

Nordheim, Arne (b. Laevik, 1931). Pioneer of electronic and avant-garde music in Norway.

Colorazione (1968, 20'), Hammond organ + percussion + electronics. Philips 854 005 AY

Epitaffio (1963, 11'), orchestra + tape (Hansen). Philips 839 250 AY

Five Osaka Fragments (1970, 19'), tape. Philips 6507 034

Respons I (1966–7), two percussion + tape. Philips 839 250 AY
Solitaire (1968, 12'), tape. Philips 6740 004, Philips 854 005 AY

Philippot, Michel (b. Verzy, 1925). Member of the Groupe de Recherches Musicales from 1959 to 1962, using *musique concrète* techniques with an unusual feeling for motivic development.
Ambiance I (1959, 7'), tape. Boîte à Musique LD 070
Ambiance II–Toast funèbre (1959, 6'), tape. Boîte à Musique LD 071
Etude I (1952, 5½'), tape. Ducretet-Thomson DUC 9, London DTL 93121
Etude III (1962, 10'), tape. Candide CE 31025, *Varèse VS 81005
Maldoror (1960, 59'), tape. Boîte à Musique LD 075–6
Rhinocéros (1960, 17'), tape. Vega T 31 SP 8003

Pousseur, Henri (b. Malmédy, Belgium, 1929). Prominent since the early fifties as avant-garde composer and theorist; co-founder in 1958 of the APELAC studio in Brussels.
Electre (1960, 48'), tape (Universal). Universal Edition UE 13500
Jeu de miroirs de Votre Faust (1966, 30½'), tape. Heliodor Wergo 2549 021, Wergo 60026
Rimes pour différentes sources sonores (1958–9, 14½'), orchestra + tape (Suvini Zerboni). RCA Victrola VICS 1239
Scambi I (1957, 6½'), tape. Limelight LS 86048, Philips 835 486 AY
Trois visages de Liège (1961, 18'), tape. *Columbia MS 7051

Powell, Mel (b. New York, NY, 1923). In 1960 founded the studio at Yale, where he used classic studio techniques in works of chamber-musical texture.
Electronic Setting I (1961, 3'), tape. Son Nova S 1
Events (1963, 7'), tape. *CRI SD 227
Second Electronic Setting (1962, 4½'), tape. *CRI SD 227

Randall, James K. (b. Cleveland, Ohio, 1929). Has worked on computer-synthesized sound at the Princeton Computer Center since 1964.
Lyric Variations (1968), violin + tape. Vanguard VCS 10057
Mudgett: Monologues by a Mass Murderer (1965, 10'), tape. *Nonesuch H 71245
Music for the film 'Eakins' (1972, 24'), tape. CRI SD 328

Quartersines (1969, 2'), tape. *Nonesuch H 71245
Quartets in Pairs (1964, 1½'), tape. * Nonesuch H 71245

Reich, Steve (b. New York, NY, 1936). Worked at the San Francisco Tape Music Center (1964–5) and then in his own studio. Since the late sixties has appeared with his own ensemble of electronic and conventional instruments, playing music based on clear rhythmic systems and bright tonal harmonies.

Come out (1966, 13½'), tape. Odyssey 32 16 0160
Four Organs (1970, 24'), four electric organs + maracas. Angel
S 36059; *Shandar 10005
It's gonna rain (1965, 17½'), tape. Columbia MS 7265
Phase Patterns (1970), four electric organs. *Shandar 10005
Violin Phase (1967), violin + tape. Columbia MS 7265

Reynolds, Roger (b. Detroit, Mich., 1934). Has involved himself since the late sixties with mixed-media works using electronics.

Ping (1968, 22'), instruments + tape + electronics + lighting.
CRI SD 285
Traces (1968–9, 23½'), instruments + tape + electronics. CRI SD
285

Riley, Terry (b. Colfax, Calif., 1935). Has worked since the mid-sixties as a composer–performer with conventional instruments and electronics, weaving meditative patterns from tonal fragments.

Dorian Reeds (1966), soprano saxophone + electronics. Mass
Art M 131
Persian Surgery Dervishes (1971, 45'), electric organ + electronics. Shanti 83 501–2
Poppy Nogood and the Phantom Band (1968, 21½'), soprano
saxophone + electronics. Columbia MS 7315
A Rainbow in Curved Air (1969, 18½'), electric keyboards.
Columbia MS 7315

Salzman, Eric (b. New York, NY, 1933). Has worked since the mid-sixties with live electronics in mixed-media works.

Helix, electronic music theatre. Finnadar 9005
Larynx Music (1967), voice + tape. Finnadar 9005
The Nude Paper Sermon (1968–9, 45'), electronic music theatre.
*Nonesuch H 71231

Queens Collage (1966), tape. Finnadar 9005
Wiretap, electronic music theatre. Finnadar 9005

Schaeffer, Pierre (b. Nancy, 1910). Invented *musique concrète* in 1948 and founded the Groupe de Musique Concrète (later Groupe de Recherches Musicales) at the RTF studios in Paris in 1951. Since the late fifties he has devoted his attention mainly to theoretical and philosophical questions rather than to composition. For joint works with Pierre Henry see above.

Etude aux allures (1958, 3½'), tape. Boîte à Musique LD 070, Philips 6521 021, Philips 6740 001
Etude aux casseroles (1948, 3½'), disc. Ducretet-Thomson DUC 8, London DTL 93090, Philips 6521 021
Etude aux chemins de fer (1948, 3'), disc. Ducretet-Thomson DUC 8, London DTL 93090, Philips 6521 021
Etude aux objets (1959, 19'), tape. Philips 835 487 AY; Philips 6521 021 (1967 version); Candide CE 31025, *Varèse VS 81005 (extract)
Etude au piano II (1948, 4'), disc. Ducretet-Thomson DUC 8, London DTL 93090
Etude aus sons animés (1958, 4½'), tape. Boîte à Musique LD 070, Philips 6521 021
Etude aux tourniquets (1948, 2'), disc. Ducretet-Thomson DUC 8, London DTL 93090, Philips 6521 021
Etude violette (1948, 3½'), disc. Philips 6521 021
L'oiseau RAI (1950, 3'), disc. Ducretet-Thomson DUC 9, London DTL 93121
Variations sur une flûte mexicaine (1949, 7½'), disc. Ducretet-Thomson DUC 8, London DTL 93090

Souster, Tim (b. Bletchley, 1943). Intermittently associated with Stockhausen since the mid-sixties; co-founder of the live electronic ensembles Intermodulation (1969–76) and 0dB (1976–), the latter leaning towards rock styles.

Afghan Amplitudes (1976, 8½'), live electronic ensemble. Transatlantic TRAG 343
Arcane Artefact (1976, 13½'), live electronic ensemble. Transatlantic TRAG 343
Music from Afar (1976, 3'), tape + electronics. Transatlantic TRAG 343

Spectral (1972, 14½'), viola + electronics. Transatlantic TRAG 343
Surfit (1976, 5'), live electronic ensemble. Transatlantic TRAG 343

Stockhausen, Karlheinz (b. Mödrath, near Cologne, 1928). A leader of musical thought since the early fifties. Much of his output is in some sense electronic, beginning with a study he composed at the Paris *musique concrète* studio in 1952. The next year he transferred to the studio at Cologne, where he has remained among the directing personnel, and where he did important work in creating music from purely electronic sources (*Studien* and *Kontakte*). Since 1964 he has toured widely with his own live electronic ensemble, and he has also explored the application of electronics to more conventional media. The creation of new sounds and new formal processes, often bringing diverse phenomena into some kind of unity, is an abiding characteristic of his music.

Aus den sieben Tagen (1968), fourteen texts for intuitive music (Universal). DGG 2720 073 ['Es' (23'), 'Aufwärts' (29'), 'Kommunion', (16½'), 'Intensität (30½'), 'Richtige Dauern' (20'), 'Verbindung' (25'), 'Unbegrenzt' (48'), 'Treffpunkt' (9½', 15½'), 'Nachtmusik' (26½'), 'Abwärts' (18'), 'Setz die Segel zur Sonne' (28½'), 'Goldstaub' (54')], DGG 2530 255 ['Es', 'Aufwärts'], DGG 2530 256 ['Kommunion', 'Intensität'], Shandar 10 002 ['Unbegrenzt']; Musique Vivante MV 30795 ['Setz die Segel zur Sonne' (21½'), 'Verbindung', (24½')]; Finnadar 9009 ['Setz die Segel zur Sonne']
Ensemble (1967, 240'), twelve instruments + electronics. Wergo 60065 (excerpts 62')
Für kommende Zeiten (1968–70), seventeen texts for intuitive music (Stockhausen). EMI Electrola C 165 02 313–4 ['Japan', 'Wach']; Chrysalis 6307 573 ['Ceylon' (25½'), 'Zugvogel' (22½')]
Gesang der Jünglinge (1955–6, 13'), tape. DGG LP 16133, *DGG 138 811
Hymnen (1966–7, 114'), tape (Universal). DGG 2707 039, DGG ST 139 421–2
Kontakte (1958–60, 34½'), tape, or piano + percussion + tape (Universal). *DGG 138 811 (tape); Wergo 60009 (+ instruments); Candide CE 31022, Vox STGBY 638 (+ instruments)
Kurzwellen (1968, 50–65'), live electronic ensemble (Universal).

DGG 139 451; DGG 139 461 ('Opus 1970', version with music by Beethoven); Finnadar 9009

Mantra (1970, 65'), two pianos + electronics (Stockhausen), *DGG 2530 208

Mikrophonie I (1964, 20–30'), tam-tam + electronics (Universal). Columbia MS 7355, CBS 72647, CBS S 77230, *DGG 2530 583

Mikrophonie II (1965, 15'), chorus + Hammond organ + electronics (Universal). Columbia MS 7355, CBS 72647, CBS S 77230, *DGG 2530 583

Mixtur (1964–7, 28'), orchestra + electronics (Universal). DGG 137 012, DGG ST 643 546

Momente (1961–72, 90'), soprano + chorus + brass + two electric organs + percussion (Universal). Nonesuch H 71157, Wergo 60024 (1965 version); DGG 2709 055 (1972 version)

Pole (1969–70), two players (Stockhausen). EMI Electrola C 165 02 313

Prozession (1967, at least 32'), live electronic ensemble (Universal). Candide CE 31001, CBS S 77230, Vox STGBY 615; Fratelli Fabbri mm 1098; DGG 2530 582

Solo (1965–6, 6–10'), player + tape delay system (Universal). DGG 137 005, DGG 104 992 (trombone version)

Spiral (1968, 15'), soloist + shortwave radio (Universal). DGG 2561 109 (oboe version); EMI Electrola C 165 02 313–14 (electronium and electrochord versions); Hör Zu SHZW 903 BL, Wergo 325 (recorder version)

Sternklang (1971, at least 180'), five groups in a park (Stockhausen). Polydor 2612 031

Studie I (1953, 9½'), tape. DGG LP 16133

Studie II (1954, 3'), tape (Universal). DGG LP 16133

Telemusik (1966, 17½'), tape (Universal). DGG 137 012, DGG ST 643 546

Trans (1971, 27'), orchestra + electronics (Stockhausen). DGG 2530 726

Ylem (1972, 22'), four electronic instruments + ensemble. DGG 2530 442

Subotnick, Morton (b. Los Angeles, Calif., 1933). Co-founder of the San Francisco Tape Music Center (1960), where he worked with Donald Buchla on the development of a synthesizer. His output includes mixed-media works as well as several colourful pieces specially composed for records on the Buchla synthesizer.

Four Butterflies, tape. Columbia M 32741

Laminations (1969), orchestra + tape. Turnabout TV 34428 S

Prelude no. 4 (1966, 17′), piano + tape. Avant 1008

Sidewinder, tape. Columbia M 30683

Silver Apples of the Moon (1967, 31½′), tape. *Nonesuch H 71174

Touch (1969), tape. Columbia MS 7316

The Wild Bull (1968, 28′), tape. Nonesuch H 71208

Ussachevsky, Vladimir (b. Hailar, Manchuria, 1911). Resident since 1930 in the USA, where he began tape experiments in 1951. He has worked closely with Otto Luening (for joint works see above), since 1959 as a director of the Columbia–Princeton Center in New York. His music shows a zestful use of classic studio techniques and, latterly, computer sound synthesis.

Computer Piece no. 1 (1968, 3½′), tape. *CRI SD 268

Conflict, tape. Folkways FTS 33904

Creation–Prologue (1960–61, 11′), four choirs + tape. Columbia MS 6566

Improvisation no. 4711 (1958, ½′), tape. Son Nova S 3

Linear Contrasts (1958, 3½′), tape. CRI S 356, Son Nova S 3

Metamorphoses (1957, 5½′), tape. CRI S 356, Son Nova S 3

Piece for Tape Recorder (1956, 5½′), tape. CRI 112, Finnadar 9010 Q

Sonic Contours (1952, 7½′), tape. Desto DC 6466

Transposition, Reverberation, Experiment, Composition (1951–2, 8′), tape. Folkways FTX 6169

Two Sketches for a Computer Piece (1971, 3½′), tape. *CRI SD 268

Underwater Valse (1952, 1′), tape. Folkways FTX 6169

Wireless Fantasy (1960, 4½′), tape. *CRI SD 227

Of Wood and Brass (1964–5, 4½′), tape. *CRI SD 227

Varèse Edgard (b. Paris, 1883; d. New York, NY, 1965). Experimented during the thirties with discs and used electronic instruments, all the while pressing for more versatile means.

Worked at studios in Paris, Eindhoven and New York during the fifties and early sixties.

Déserts (1949–54, 23½'), orchestra + tape (Colombo). Columbia MS 6362; *CRI SD 268

Ecuatorial (1934, 12'), bass + orchestra including two ondes martenot (Colombo). Nonesuch H 71269; Vanguard VCS 10047

Poème électronique (1957–8, 8'), tape. *Columbia MS 6146

Wuorinen, Charles (b. New York, NY, 1938). Prolific composer for conventional forces, combining serial organization with a strong sense of musical gesture. His only important tape piece, below, was composed with the RCA Synthesizer.

Time's Encomium (1968–9, 31½'), tape. *Nonesuch H 71225

Xenakis, Iannis (b. Braïla, Romania, 1922). Resident since 1947 in Paris, where he has worked occasionally at the French radio studio. His works show a skilled handling of sound masses, sometimes generated with the aid of computer calculation.

Analogique B (1958–9, 2½'), tape. Philips 835 487 AY

Bohor (1962, 22'), tape. Erato STU 70530, *Nonesuch H 71246

Concret PH (1958, 3'), tape. Philips 835 487 AY; Erato STU 70530, *Nonesuch H 71246 (revised version, 1968)

Diamorphoses (1957–8, 7'), tape. Boîte à Musique LD 070; Erato STU 70530, *Nonesuch H 71246 (revised version, 1968)

Orient-occident (1960, 11'), tape. Limelight LS 86047, Philips 835 485 AY; Erato STU 70530, *Nonesuch H 71246 (revised version, 1968)

Persepolis (1971), tape. Philips 6521 045

Young, LaMonte (b. Bern, Idaho, 1935). Since 1962 has been concerned with the creation of long, drone-based sound environments, often with electronic means.

13 I 73 5:35–6:14:03 PM NYC (1969–73, 39'), performers + electronics. Shandar 83 510

Drift Study 14 VII 73 9:27:27–10:06:41 PM NYC (1973, 39'), tuned sine tones. Shandar 83 510

Included here is a small selection of records which are particularly interesting for their display of electronic techniques.

The Beach Boys: *Smiley Smile* (1966–7). Capitol T 2891

The Beatles: *Revolver* (1966). Parlophone PCS 7009

——: *Sgt Pepper's Lonely Hearts Club Band* (1967). Capitol MAS 2653, Parlophone PCS 7027

Emerson, Lake and Palmer: *Brain Salad Surgery* (1973). Manticore MC 66669

Brian Eno: *Another Green World* (1975). Island ILPS 9351

——: *Discreet Music* (1975). Obscure 3

Edgar Froese: *Aqua* (1973–4). Virgin V 2016, Virgin VR 13 111

The Grateful Dead: *Anthem of the Sun* (1967–8). Warner Brothers WS 1749

——: *Aoxomoxoa* (1969). Warner Brothers WS 1790

——: *Live/Dead* (1968). Warner Brothers WS 1830

Jimi Hendrix: *The Jimi Hendrix Experience* (1967–8). Polydor 2683 031, Reprise RS 6261

Patrick Moraz: *I* (1976). Atlantic SD 18175

Mike Oldfield: *Tubular Bells* (1975). Virgin V 2001

Pink Floyd: *The Dark Side of the Moon* (1972–3). EMI Harvest SHVL 804

Tangerine Dream: *Cyclone* (1978). Virgin V 2097

Velvet Underground: *Andy Warhol's Velvet Underground Featuring Nico* (1967–9). MGM 2683 006

Yes: *Close to the Edge* (1972). Atlantic K 50012, Atlantic SD 7244

Frank Zappa: *Uncle Meat* (1967–8). Bizarre 2024

III.2   Glossary

amplifier. A device to increase the strength of an electrical signal, in order that the signal may, for example, cause a loudspeaker to vibrate.

amplitude. The strength of a signal (musical or, more commonly, electrical), as measured physically; the equivalent physiological dimension is that of loudness.

amplitude modulation. The variation of amplitude, usually by electronic means. For example, the effect of slow, regular amplitude modulation is to produce a tremolo.

ARP. A common variety of synthesizer.

band. A continuous range of frequencies.

Buchla. A common variety of synthesizer, invented and developed by Donald Buchla.

colour. *See* timbre.

coloured noise. A variety of noise (q.v.) having an uneven distribution of frequencies.

cycle. The repeating unit in the wave form of a signal.

cycles per second. Commonly used as a measurement of frequency; abbreviated as c.p.s.

decibel. The standard unit for describing relative loudnesses of sounds; abbreviated dB.

digital. Handling information not continuously but in discrete 'bits', rather as a film camera takes an image of reality in separate frames.

digital-to-analog converter. An electronic device which converts digital information into an analog, or continuous, output. Used in computer sound synthesis to convert the output of a digital computer into a form which can be reproduced as sound.

Elektronische Musik. Term coined at Cologne in the early fifties to distinguish electronically synthesized music from *musique concrète*.

envelope. The shape of a sound in time; the term is normally used to denote variation in amplitude from start to extinction.

envelope generator. An electronic device, usually included in synthesizers, which gives a particular envelope to a sound.

equalizer. An electronic device which increases the contribution of a certain frequency range in a sound.

filter. An electronic device which decreases the contribution of a certain frequency range in a sound. A 'band-reject' filter eliminates a defined band, while a 'band-pass' filter eliminates all but a defined band.

formant. A range of frequencies which is characteristic of a particular timbre. We recognize vowel sounds, for example, because each has formants which remain the same despite other variations in vocal quality.

frequency. The rate of fluctuation in a signal; the equivalent physiological dimension is that of pitch.

frequency modulation. The variation of frequency, usually by electronic means. The effect of slow, regular frequency modulation is to produce a vibrato.

graphic notation. Musical notation using other than traditional symbols. The graphics may indicate musical events (e.g. a curved line to show a smooth change in pitch) or they may be merely suggestive.

GROOVE. A computer program for the generation of sound in real time, enabling the musician to 'play' a computer as he would a conventional instrument.

harmonic. A component in a sound having a frequency which is a common multiple of that of the fundamental. For example, the harmonics of A = 440 c.p.s. are A = 880 c.p.s., E = 1320 c.p.s., A = 1760 c.p.s., C$\sharp$ = 2200 c.p.s., etc.

Hertz. Alternative nomenclature for the unit of frequency; abbreviated Hz. 1 Hz = 1 c.p.s.

inharmonic. Containing frequency components which are not harmonics of the fundamental. The greater the inharmonicity, the greater the clangorousness of the sound.

intermodulation. Term introduced by Stockhausen in the mid-sixties to denote the causing, by electronic means, of two or more sounds to interfere with each other.

loudspeaker. A device which converts electrical into sound signals.

microphone. A device which converts sound into electrical signals, which may then be amplified, recorded, etc. A 'contact microphone' is affixed to the sounding body; an 'air microphone' picks up vibrations from the air.

mixer. A device which combines electrical signals.

modulation. Electronic interference between signals. *See also* amplitude modulation, frequency modulation, intermodulation, ring modulation.

Moog. A common variety of synthesizer, invented and developed by Robert Moog. The word is properly pronounced with a long *o* as in 'vogue'.

MUSIC V. A computer program for sound synthesis, introduced by Max Mathews and subsequently adapted by others.

musique concrète. Tape music created from recordings of natural, as opposed to electronically generated, sounds.

noise. Sound without definite pitch; *see also* coloured noise, white noise.

ondes martenot. An electronic musical instrument invented in the twenties by Maurice Martenot.

potentiometer. An electronic device for varying voltage. In electronic music, potentiometers can vary loudness, pitch, etc.

pulse. A single burst of electricity or sound. A 'pulse wave' is a regular succession of pulses.

RCA Synthesizer. A sound-generating apparatus developed in the fifties; the unique Mark II model is at the Columbia–Princeton Center for Electronic Music in New York.

real time. Time as it passes. Used to distinguish activities which give results as they are accomplished (e.g. playing the piano) from those which do not (e.g. preparing a piece of tape music).

reverberation. Echo which cannot be distinguished from the original sound, to which it gives a continuing aura.

ring modulation. The electronic combination of two signals to produce an output containing only sum and difference frequencies. For example, if the signals are sine waves of 200 c.p.s. and 300 c.p.s., the output will contain frequencies of 100 c.p.s. and 500 c.p.s. The process often results in a harshening of sound due to the inharmonicity of the product.

sequencer. An electronic device which can store and reproduce a cycle of voltages. When used with a synthesizer it can give rise to an ostinato pattern or to more complex effects.

signal. A sound or, more usually, its electrical representation: thus a microphone may be said to convert a sound into a signal.

sine tone. A sound containing only one frequency.

sine wave. The smoothly undulating wave form of a sine tone.

square wave. A symmetrical, crenellated wave form; the equivalent sound has a buzzy quality.

synthesizer. An electronic musical instrument using voltage-controlled devices and often very versatile in its capabilities.

Synthi. A common variety of synthesizer.

tape. Plastic material coated with metallic oxides which can store magnetic patterns representing sounds.

tape recorder. An electronic device for storing signals on tape and reproducing them.

tape music. Term coined by Luening and Ussachevsky in the early fifties to denote music composed on tape.

theremin. An electronic musical instrument developed between the wars by Leon Termen or Thérémin.

timbre. That quality of sound which is characteristic of, for instance, a particular variety of instrument, so that one may speak of 'clarinet timbre' or 'horn timbre'. Differences of timbre arise from differences in the spectra of frequency components in sounds.

transient. An unrepeated feature of a sound. For example, a 'starting transient' may differ markedly from the sustained tone which follows it in the case, say, of a violin sound.

trautonium. An electronic musical instrument invented in the twenties by Friedrich Trautwein.

VCS. A common variety of synthesizer.

voltage control. The control of electronic devices by electrical means, rather than manually.

white noise. Noise in which, theoretically, all frequency components are present at the same intensity.

Bibliography

General texts

Appleton, Jon, and Perera, Ronald, eds: *The Development and Practice of Electronic Music* (Englewood Cliffs, NJ, 1975)

Beauchamp, James, and von Forester, Heinz, eds: *Music by Computers* (New York, 1969)

Cross, Lowell: *A Bibliography of Electronic Music* (Toronto, 1967, rev. 1968)

Davies, Hugh, ed.: *Répertoire international des musiques électroacoustiques/International Electronic Music Catalog* (Cambridge, Mass., 1968)

Ernst, David: *The Evolution of Electronic Music* (New York, 1977)

Lincoln, Harry, ed.: *The Computer and Music* (Ithaca, NY, 1970)

Nyman, Michael: *Experimental Music: Cage and Beyond* (London, 1974)

Russcol, Herbert: *The Liberation of Sound* (Englewood Cliffs, NJ, 1972)

Schwartz, Elliott: *Electronic Music: a Listener's Guide* (New York, 1973; London, 1973)

Practical manuals

Howe, Hubert S.: *Electronic Music Synthesis* (New York, 1975; London, 1975)

Judd, Frederick: *Electronic Music and Musique Concrète* (London, 1961)

Mathews, Max V.: *The Technology of Computer Music* (Cambridge, Mass., 1969)

Strange, Allan: *Electronic Music* (Dubuque, Iowa, 1972)

Trythall, Gilbert: *Principles and Practice of Electronic Music* (New York, 1973)

Books by or on particular composers

Cage, John: *Silence* (Middletown, Conn., 1961)

———: *A Year from Monday* (Middletown, Conn., 1967)

Charbonnier, Georges: *Entretiens avec Edgard Varèse* (Paris, 1970)

Cott, Jonathan: *Stockhausen: Conversations with the Composer* (New York, 1973; London, 1974)

Heikinheimo, Seppo: *The Electronic Music of Karlheinz Stockhausen*, Acta Musicologica Fennica vi (Helsinki, 1972)

Hiller, Lejaren, and Isaacson, Leonard: *Experimental Music* (New York, 1959)

Kostelanetz, Richard, ed.: *John Cage* (New York, 1970; London, 1971)

Maconie, Robin: *The Works of Karlheinz Stockhausen* (London, 1976)

Pousseur, Henri: *Fragments théoriques*, 2 vols (Brussels, 1970, 1972)

Schaeffer, Pierre: *A la recherche d'une musique concrète* (Paris, 1952)

———: *Traité des objets musicaux* (Paris, 1966)

Stockhausen, Karlheinz: *Texte*, 4 vols (Cologne, 1963, 1964, 1971, 1978)

Wörner, Karl H.: *Stockhausen: Life and Work* (Berkeley, Calif., 1973; London, 1973)

Periodicals

Electronic Music Review, 1–7 (1967–9)

Journal of Music Theory, i- (1957–)

Perspectives of New Music, i- (1962–)

Die Reihe, 1–8 (1955–62, Eng. trans., 1958–68)

Source, 1–9 (1967–71)

Index

References to the list of recordings are given for composers only, and are printed in italic.